embrace
that
girl

Erica,
I can't wait to
create some magic
w/ you on Thrive ♡
love & light,
Cris

cris ramos greene

embrace that girl

a love story

with the girl in the mirror

These are my memories, from my perspective, and I have tried to represent events as faithfully as possible. Some scenarios in this book are fictitious. Any similarity to actual persons, living or dead, is coincidental.

ISBN: 978-1-7351662-0-9

Edited by Anne Maynard, Sarah Miles and Jaime Greene
Cover design by Paula Guerrero
Layout by Lynn Everard

thecrisramos.com

The dedication of this book is split 7 ways.

To my sweetheart and soulmate, Jaime. *Te quiero mucho amor mio. Es una burrada.*

To my parents who gave me everything. I love you both infinitely.

To Steph, my Scorpio queen, my mirror and my opposite.

To Cris and Cam, my sisters and best friends in this life and many others.

To you, dear reader, and your journey. May you embrace every single delicious part of yourself. You deserve it.

Contents

1   Finding my amazing life   1

2   *Un clavo saca otro clavo*   9

3   A generation of G chat employees   23

4   Katy Perry, a nun and Julia Roberts walk into a bar   33

5   That time I went to a psychic   45

6   My first adult apartment   55

7   Deadlines and boy glow   69

8   The call   77

9   Game Changer   93

10   The Golden Opportunity you are seeking is within you   105

11   Confetti confession   123

12   Revelations of reemployment   131

13   Show me yours, I'll show you mine   143

14   A new beginning   153

15   Bad news bears   167

16   Don't take it all so seriously   175

17   Embrace That Girl   191

Dear reader,

The following is based on a true story. Names have been
changed, except my own, to protect the privacy and anonymity
of each person who touched my life. All of the insights are fully
mine, even, and especially, the ugly ones.

So often we can be unreliable narrators, telling the world one
story about ourselves all the while missing who we truly are. It's
not until we look under the hood years later that we understand.

I invite you to look underneath mine.

c.

1
Finding my amazing life

There's pee on the floor. I still don't know why or how a woman could possibly miss the pot, but the evidence is there, glistening right between my shoes. It's not the first time I've performed a careful balancing act in a restroom to avoid stepping in pee while life's bigger questions loom in my head. But today, I'm sober and this isn't a bathroom in a bar, making this a decisive first.

On the other side of the stall door, a maid complains in Spanish about a guest who has wet the hotel bed.

"*Tiene que ser orina*," she says casually to her co-worker on the walkie talkie as she sprays the counter. She's seen this before, "*probablemente orinaron justo en el colchón.*" Has to be pee, they probably did it right on the mattress.

As I zip up and open the door, she smiles widely, unfazed by my presence. She either assumes I don't speak Spanish or that I know what to expect in a place like this, an old hotel chain located directly outside Miami International Airport. It's a rough area, not the sort of place that comes to mind when most people think of Miami, a tourist destination known for luxury. In many ways, places like this are the real Miami. They're the areas people pass by without notice so they can get distracted by all the glitter.

I catch a glimpse of myself in the smudged mirror above the sink. My face looks chapped in the harsh lighting of this small windowless bathroom. I wash my hands and go through the motions, making peace with why I'm here. To transform. To change. To experience a breakthrough. Although I've read all the books on changing myself, this time is different. I'm thirty now, it's time to get my shit together. As I follow the signs left thoughtfully right outside the bathroom, I find a large group of people in line. Bingo.

I'm at a seminar in a nondescript, broken down hotel giving me little hope I will experience a breakthrough in its "ballroom." The garish green pattern on the carpeted floor makes me dizzy as I drink the crappy free coffee they serve for guests only. I guess I technically am a guest although I'm not staying the night. I'll be here for the next four full days leaving at midnight to drive home, or so the tentative schedule on the pamphlet says. It's all subject to change. How did I get here? I wonder as I turn to my fiancé. He's not fazed by the dungeon we're sitting in, but the eight pages of NDA forms we have to carefully read and fill out have him on edge. I can see his eyes scrunch up every so often as he pauses, lets out a sigh and signs his name as if he's rolling his eyes.

A month ago, our friend Melanie took this course and convinced us to sign up. I'd been observing her behavior. She was different. I couldn't put my finger on exactly how but she seemed to possess a presence and knowledge that wasn't there before. I asked her what had changed and her eyes lit up excitedly telling me about a training that changed her life. I was all in after a few conversations, but I had some things to work out before I could sign on the dotted line: find a way to pay for it and convince my fiancé.

The weeks kept passing me by until one day I got into my car after work, the same white Honda Accord my dad gave me in high school, leaving my job after witnessing a grown man have a tantrum in front of a group of people. How did I get here? The familiar question came up again, as it has during many moments of my life. Grown people having tantrums had shockingly become a normal part of my workday, but this wasn't supposed to be a permanent job. I gripped the wheel of my old trusted car, which was balding from 10 years of gripping and looking out at the road in front of me planning for a future that's never come.

Dozens of brake lights from the backs of stopped cars stared at me on the same road I'd been taking every day after work. I had my routine down to the minute: turn on my maps app to be sure 7th Avenue is the fastest route, which it always was, shut it off and stay on the road until I hang a left on the overpass. That's when the real traffic starts. But that day the traffic began sooner, and I was stopped on 7th Avenue, which was under construction. Who the hell is building this thing? Shouldn't it be done? Not that I know anything about road construction, but I had the time, so I calculated in my head how long it had been when a scary realization sank in. Construction started right after I began this job as a temp. It had been under construction for two years. Two fucking years.

I called Melanie so we could meet and talk about the training that night because I knew then I needed something. By the end of our conversation, I was all in, captivated by the promise of becoming the best version of myself, finally, or maybe even someone completely different. My fiancé, however, required some convincing.

We both sat in our apartment, wine in hand, giving it our best argument. I went with the, why not? What's the worst that could happen? I also pointed out to him the many moments he described to me of being stuck in traffic, his commute far worse than mine, and wondering what the fuck he was doing with his life.

"I see your point, but... this kind of sounds like a cult," he crossed his arms, a bad sign for team training.

Melanie, who had an advantage since she underwent

whatever magic happened to people at these things, wasn't deterred by his resistance. She listened intently to him.

"I completely understand your reservations, but you have a really strong mind. You would never be brainwashed by a cult. Don't you trust yourself?"

He seemed a bit more loose. "Well, maybe Cris should do it first. If we do it, I think we should do it separately so we could each have our own experience."

Again, she waited until the very last word he said before she nodded her head no. "I did it separately from my boyfriend and I don't recommend it. Trust me, it'll be better for you both as a couple to do it together. The things you can accomplish as a team after the training," her arms went up showing us the magnitude of possibility. "And while you'll be in it together, you won't really be together. So, don't worry, you will be in independent experiences. That's all I can say."

We signed up for it that night.

I immediately felt better. Though nothing had happened yet, the false sense of accomplishment I feel when I intend to do something I want but haven't actually done yet, set in. The weeks leading up to this day felt light and carefree, brimming with promises of an alternate universe where I am a new me. But now I'm here signing my rights away and agreeing to follow a long list of rules, and it feels differently than I expected. For one thing, we are not to drink water inside the training room under any circumstances unless given permission. Now that I see the dimly lit ballroom that is our "training room," it seems a bit odd to only hydrate outside. Are they afraid we'll get anything on the garish green carpet? Or, is this a ploy to dehydrate us, therefore putting us in a weaker state that will make us more impressionable? I'm sobering up to the fact that I haven't done any of the work and maybe, just maybe, this is a goddamn cult.

My fiancé looks at me and puffs his cheeks as he clicks his pen showing me the stack of forms he's completed. It's his version of miming: I told you so.

4

The program trainers say things like, "There are no coincidences," as they pick up our papers and run our credit cards. I've tried crazier things in the name of changing myself. Hell, I've sat down before several mystics, all reputable in their craft, searching for the same answers I hope to get here. I've poured cold water with white petals over my naked body in the shower just before journaling and lighting the pages aflame in my trash bin, which I'm sure was a fire hazard. I think that thing was plastic. All of this to say, I've tried some shit and made every effort I could think of to understand who I am, and even better who I could be. And don't we all do some version of this? The self-development sections at the bookstores grow a little more every year. I scroll through my Instagram and it seems everyone is trying to be a self-help influencer. It's never been more popular to want to be better. Years ago, it was cheesy and a little embarrassing, like online dating. But now I'm hard pressed not to find a closeted self-improver. We all secretly light our trash bins ablaze affirming all kinds of things to ourselves. Does this sound psycho to you yet? Or, are you as intrigued as the rest of us?

The feeling of letting go, of getting over myself enough to be in this situation— a sitcom scenario at best or an embarrassing revelation of my insecurities at worst— is what I'm trying to accept right now as I ignore whether or not I'm thirstier than I've ever been in my life because I actually need water or because I can't drink it inside. My fiancé looks at me strangely because I keep sucking my saliva.

Truth is, I have no way to tell you if this training will work or if I'm any better than these people seated alongside me all seemingly less thirsty. All I can tell you is my story of being committed to mastering my relationship with myself by any means necessary. So, I'm here to find out. It's why I'm willing to try this transformational training even though my excitement has slowly changed to suspicion and part of me keeps looking at the trainers like they're coming out any minute with Kool Aid to quench our thirst.

From my safe seat in the back of the room, I can observe the rest of the people pouring in. Some people look like they really need this, while others make me wonder why they're here. The assumed cries for help are the odd-looking folks, like the girl who is a little too loud and wearing about eighteen different shades of pink, or the tall dude wearing an all-black cowboy outfit even though it's August in Miami, his long thinning ponytail topped off by a noticeable bald spot when he removes his hat. And then there are the alphas, like the handsome blonde dude who looks as if he's in his mid-twenties and walked right out of an Abercrombie catalog, or another older woman that immediately introduced herself to me and five others with a power handshake explaining she's traveled here from her second home in upstate New York. She's a successful entrepreneur with an impeccable white pixie cut and shimmery diamond earrings. I wonder which group I belong in. Do they think I really need this or am I a question mark? Am I as transparent as they are?

The forms indicated we dress casually but I'm from Miami, so my concept of casual is designer jeans and a slinky white tee dressed up with a summer scarf, which is coming in handy because this ballroom is freezing. Why are ballrooms always so cold? I wonder if they set the temperature low as a form of psychological control, maybe we're more vulnerable because a good portion of our brain is spending its energy warming our body.

The room gets quiet as our orator walks on stage. He's handsome in a nerdy way, probably in his thirties. His suit is too big and an ugly shade of beige, which sort of matches with the aging vanilla wallpaper in our modest training room. His hair is slicked to the side with gel, its shiny, jet black hue contrasts nicely with his milky white skin. He's attractive in a clean-cut sort of way. And then he begins to yell at us.

"Why are you here?" It's less of a question and more of an accusation.

His blue eyes pierce my soul right through his glasses. One by one, he makes eye contact with everyone in the room.

"Because you've gotten comfortable. Well let me tell you something." He lowers his voice for effect and adjusts his wedding ring right before he lands his hook, "Comfort arrives as a guest, stays as a host and remains to enslave you."

He lets that sit in the air as we all presumably take a scan of our lives and decide to trust him. Yes, it's true. Comfort has been an unwelcome guest keeping me in a strange purgatory, a state that's not exactly painful but not joyful. What I mean to say is, my life is good with short bursts of greatness, but mostly filled with days that feel like the real things I want are out of my reach.

"Isn't that why you're here?" he says coolly, going back to good cop in a way I can tell he's practiced before, a slightly aggressive tough-love approach directly followed by his casual I'm-your-pal persona.

"We can create anything in our lives from nothing by simply declaring it so," he finishes and stands in silence once more to give the crowd time to consider if we're in or out.

The rest of the group, oddballs and alphas alike, are all smiling captivated. They're in. I keep scanning the room in awe at the effect this man has. It's incredible and yet a tad frightening. Being here and forced to confront my discomfort is not the same as reading books at home, no matter how life altering the content is. I take a deep breath and decide to trust my initial instinct to be here. Fuck it. I'm in too.

As the speaker asks us to consider what brought us here, I think back. There are all the obvious things, like the fact that I just turned 30 and have a stagnant career. There's my low self-esteem and in general my need to be approved by others. No doubt there's some family stuff. While they love and support me, there is a significant barrier in our relationship, namely that I'm rational.

But, to his point, what really brought me here? That's a longer story. If I had to consider his question thoughtfully, it all began when I entered the "real world," or whatever version of that people like to talk about when referring to becoming an adult. Ever since I graduated from college and entered the workforce, I've been failing to feel like an accomplished person. I've come closer for sure, but I thought I'd be a lot farther at thirty.

I agree with him that comfort has never really been on my side. I don't like feeling out of control, not even a little bit. I've held onto beliefs, relationships and behaviors that should have been phases in my life for so long after their expiration date it's laughable. My own stagnation is not unlike the 7th Avenue construction. I've been showing up in my hard hat and banging random things with tools bolstered by the prospect of a finished product, only it never seems to get here. Years pass and then I find myself rinsing and recycling the same long-term goals never quite making the stride I need to get there.

What lies on the other side of my comfort? I really hope it's my freedom.

2

Un clavo saca otro clavo

7 years earlier

We have a saying in Spanish, *un clavo saca otro clavo*. It literally translates to, one nail removes another, and we use it when speaking about the things that worry us. It means something new has replaced something old, and it is helping us absolve the pain of the old wound.

That is how I find myself in an apartment right outside Madrid. Everyone is still asleep, it's 8:30 AM. I'm having my second cup of coffee and sitting by the open window with my journal. There are some kids playing in their pool, and save for their voices off in the distance, all I can hear is the slight whistling of a summer breeze. The coffee here tastes different from the one I drink back home. I don't know what it is exactly, but I like it.

I'm on an unexpected trip driven by two different forces of nature. At the beginning of the summer I'd never have guessed this is where I'd be, in love, in Spain, but here I am. I've thrown myself all in with total abandon because I needed it. This is the first force of nature that brings me here. Just two short months ago my heart was torn apart, broken beyond repair. I was dry

9

heaving from the grief that marked the final ending of my first great love. It felt like a nail driven straight through my chest.

Adan is the nail removing the one painfully lodged like a stake through my heart. He is that levity, he is a healing presence and his way of being is so foreign. His playfulness and courageousness replaced the heaviness of a relationship that felt dark and guarded. I'm at the midway point of our trip and suppressing the anguish building in my stomach at the thought of leaving him here. I wake up extra early to write these feelings down and email my friend Cassandra, since I cannot say them to Adan or my sister Sofi, who is traveling with me.

Sofi is the second force of nature that conspired to bring me here. I already took my European backpacking adventure midway through my college career. That's where I met Cassandra and began the tradition of writing long letters to each other whenever either one of us is in Europe. In just one more semester I graduate, and God knows what I'll do then. Sofi, however, is at her midway point, which I envy. This is her summer and she had her own version of a big European exploration planned. She was due to backpack her way through several points in Spain and two weeks before the trip, her friend dropped out... leaving one slot vacant for a person willing to forego their summer plans for a month and make the trek with her.

When she called me panicking, I was in my apartment in Gainesville with Adan curled up under a blanket.

"Oh no, she dropped out?" I said as Adan's face came up from his phone immediately. "That really sucks. You already have your ticket? Shoot. Well, I gotta go but keep me posted."

"Go with her," he said right as the phone hung up.

"Really? But I want to spend the summer with you," I said holding his hand knowing our time was already borrowed.

"I'll be moved into Spain by those dates, come visit me. You can help me settle in and make sure someone is providing your sister with an essential college experience."

I laughed, "Well, I guess I have to, right? It's the public servant in me."

And here we are.

"Hey," Sofi says, startling me. I didn't know she was up. "I'm ready." She's holding a box of hair dye. Fuck.

Just three days ago, in a move of great haste, my sister bought a bottle of black hair dye at a shop in a small town on the outskirts of Madrid, not far from Adan's apartment. The store was stocked with items that weren't just expired but looked as if they were part of a museum. It was a collection of artifacts from another generation still preserved and even more remarkable: on sale. This is where she felt absolutely certain her next hair color was, directly next to a pack of purple scrunchies.

She motions for me to meet her in the bathroom. It's go time.

"Do you think if I mix the black and blonde in it will get lighter?" she sticks her head out the shower, her big brown eyes staring right at me more accusingly than inquisitively.

"We won't know until we try it," I hand her another bottle.

Adan walks in singing loudly in narration of his entrance. He does this. He sings what he's doing, and not just with humming, full-on lyrics. I know the song will be over when he begins to drop the beat and belt out a last line. Today, he's chosen to end with the familiar middle school notes of R&B.

"Papers and books put awaayyyaaa and that's my dayyyaaaa. Hey charm charm puffs," he kisses me on the forehead.

"Christ on a cross. I don't know how the hell I haven't shot myself yet," Sofi's muffled voice echoes from inside the shower.

Admittedly, I am not the best of partners to have stepped in on this particular trip, though beggars can't be choosers. She booked the trip with another single girl on the eve of her second serious breakup. I knew all too well what those wounds tasted like and I know it all turns out exactly as it should, but I don't offer her this advice. As a person in love, it comes off condescending, so instead I ask Adan to find another viable male presence to accompany us tonight.

"Hi Sofi!" he yells into her general direction.

"Hey Adan!"

"How was your morning?" I ask.

"I learned how to say all the muscles in my arm in Spanish!" he sings, showing me his arm.

"Well that's fun. Hey, what are we doing tonight?"

"We are all going to an Irish bar. We're meeting Jacob there around 7. How does that homeslice?" he yells to my sister.

"Sounds gooood," she says scrubbing away. I can see black streaks in the water at the foot of the shower. It's working.

"What's he doing here?" I knew Jacob by face. He was around in high school. I wondered if he was scattered around Spain studying abroad like some of our friends were.

"He's visiting family," Adan says and gives me a kiss.

"Oh cool. Okay, well, out you go. We gotta concentrate," I kiss him again and shut the bathroom door. "Jacob's cute, by the way, so there's that."

"Cris, he has a girlfriend, but I will take this life vest because if that man calls you sugar worms or some other dumbass name while he gazes into your eyes and I have to see it alone, I swear I will chug this entire bottle of hair dye."

It's true. Jacob's presence is needed. He's a relatively unknown dude who could possibly be dull and will certainly not be my sister's summer fling, but I'm still eternally thankful for this man. Tonight, my sister will not be the third at our table-for-two.

We follow the instructions step-by-step. It's time to dry it. The damage is done. There's no going back now. As the blow dryer does its job, her hair begins to reveal its new color. It's so dark it shines purple. I don't dare say it out loud, so I silently make a new rule: never, ever touch your hair when you are depressed or bored.

"It looks good," I say.

She merely blinks.

***

Dozens of underpriced beers and cocktails later, we're feeling lightheaded and ordering the way people do when hangovers have not yet been taken into careful consideration. I notice Jacob's soft-spoken voice and tanned skin; he's not my type of handsome, but handsome he is. Not a bad shoe-in for male company.

"There's this book you have to read," Jacob says. He puts down his beer, speaking excitedly with his hands. He does this a lot I'm noticing. "It will change the way you see death. It will radically alter the way you see life!"

"Do you believe in reincarnation?" I say a little too hopefully.

"I'm certain of it," he looks me straight in the eyes like he knows something I don't.

"I think so too, how else do you explain deja vu? Or getting along with certain people right away? There has to be more to it than we just got here and it all ends when we go!" I am raising my glass to prove my point.

He nods in agreement while rolling a cigarette. "Of course. It only makes sense the people you get along with the most have traveled in past lives with you. God, you've got to read this book, and tell me when you do!" he points at me with his one available finger as he seals his hand-rolled cigarette with a lick.

Adan and Sofi look bored as hell, so we finish our drinks and move on to our next stop, a hookah bar that's practically empty. I don't quite understand its theme. There are red neon lights over each table, Hookahs donning Arabic letters and what appears to be Hawaiian-type flowers and decor on the walls. Each thing looks displaced but the whole of it oddly works together. It evokes the strange visual stew of a scene right out of a Quentin Tarantino movie.

A young woman with short pink hair and a nose ring

approaches us. She looks bored as she hands us a giant menu with different cocktails and hookah flavors. Jacob grabs one and immediately starts ordering from her.

"Strawberry and mint okay?" he says.

"Yeah!" Adan gets his second wind back. "Let's go get shots, homeslice." He taps my sister on the leg. I love that he takes care of her.

"Great idea! This round is on me, but buyer's choice," she raises her eyebrows and grabs her purse.

"So, this is random," I say.

Our bored server is back and inserts the strawberry and mint flavor into our Hookah.

"Gracias," Jacob says. "Tell me," he nods at me as he tests the flavors taking small puffs and letting out little O's.

"What about ghosts? Do you believe in the whole trapped spirits thing, or maybe just maybe, it's dimensions crossing. Like they're not haunting us but we're overlapping because-"

"Time is not linear," he finishes for me, letting out a cough and handing me the hose. "That's super interesting. I've never thought about it that way, actually. It's more logical than these people sticking around with unfinished business."

Strawberry and mint fill my lungs as I exhale a big cloud of smoke. The room begins to get a little hazy now that we have the hookah going.

"Shots!" Adan and my sister arrive with four very large pink shots. Oh God.

"Don't ask what it is," Jacob puts his hand on my shoulder.

"To new friends in Spain!" Sofi proclaims.

"To new friends!"

"Hey, I feel like I'm in Alice and Wonderland or something with these lights," I say to Adan.

"Yeah, super trippy huh?" he blows a bit of smoke and then takes a sip of his whiskey.

Everything is filtered with the glow of red lights. I'd only ever seen something like that when I was backpacking through Amsterdam with Cassandra. I remember walking down the narrow streets of the Red Light District and watching women with all kinds of bodies on display in their little boxes waiting for people to pay them for sex. It was like a giant vending machine only there were humans inside. One woman looked so bored, she sat smoking while reading a magazine. She could tell we were just onlookers and didn't even care that the unflattering angle she sat in made the flesh of her tummy spill over her thong. I guess it didn't really matter. I wanted to see what color eyes she had. I couldn't tell under the red glow. It's weird how the red lights do that. Even now, we all look like we have beady eyes. I stare into Adan's, which I know are moss green, but I cannot tell. I can't see the green or the little specks of brown on his iris, only one big beady eye.

"You switched to whiskey?" I can hear a slight slur developing.

"Yeah, that Guinness got a bit heavy," Adan says and moves a piece of my hair away from my face.

"That's gonna hurt tomorrow," I tap his head.

He chugs the rest, "Totally worth it. 'Nother one?"

"Yeah, why not?" I say and take another huff.

Jacob and my sister are cracking up. Good. She needs it.

"What's so funny?" I ask.

"Your sister is a Mother Fuckin' Gangsta, that's what's so funny," Jacob says taking the hose from me. He takes a big inhale and lets it all out, "So tiny and yet so tough."

Sofi is laughing and it's the most I've seen her let go during this trip.

"I was telling him about that girl I had to put in her place in Barcelona," she rolled her eyes. It still stung her a little.

That was our stop before this last stretch in Madrid. We had been shimmying through a club and I accidentally stepped on some girl, who proceeded to shove me rudely. When my sister saw, she moved me aside and pushed the girl so hard she tripped.

"What's your problem?" the girl yelled over the music.

"Don't push people," she said pointing to me.

"Hey, she fell into ME," she emphasized that last part.

"Well don't come to a fucking club if you want personal space!" The girl backed down. Maybe what my sister said made sense or maybe she knew who she could push and who she couldn't. Either way, Jacob is right. My sister is an unexpected package of a person. She only knows life in excess. She is very petite, even smaller than me at 5'1. Everything about her expressions are an exaggeration. Nothing just happens to my sister, it's the worst or the best thing ever. This is either really good or really bad if you're around her.

"Shots!" Adan yells and I see four large questionably colored shots come our way.

"What color is that?" I ask no one in particular.

"Who cares bitch! The color of freedom," she hands each of us the giant cup of brown liquid.

And then we start a customary chant, which is a Cuban saying from back in Miami, *"Para arriba, para abajo, para el centro, para dentro!"* Our glasses do the dance of this age-old drinking song: It goes up, it goes down, it goes to the center, it goes in!

And that's the last thing I remember.

***

The next morning Sofi is in a better mood than usual. I can hear her putting away her couch bed and singing from the living room. She really needed human interaction outside of our love bubble.

"Morning pancakes," Adan kisses me on the forehead and goes to make us coffee. I get out of bed and immediately fall cross legged on the floor. The entire room is spinning violently.

"Fuck we have a flight to catch tomorrow," I murmur.

"It's just a hangover, you'll be fine by tomorrow," Sofi says walking in to help me get up. "Shower, you'll feel better."

The shower's water does make me feel better. I can feel the beads flowing down my face and slowly it heals my pounding head, or maybe that's the Advil? Whatever. I soap up around my belly, which is bloated from salty Spanish food, Guinness and mystery shots.

And then I feel something else in my stomach, sadness. My eyes scrunch up as if that'll expel it. Cris, you knew this would happen. He's living in Spain, what did you think this moment would feel like? Well, not like this. I wasn't thinking. I threw my heart into this love like there wasn't a possibility it would end. I didn't think and now I'm here.

The door opens and Adan sticks his head in, "Making breakfast for you! The healing powers of eggs and Jamón Serrano await!" he sings and shuts the door. I hear him and my sister laughing. I want this moment to last forever. Why do I have to go back to my dorm? Why can't I say fuck it and move here?

You know why. And all of a sudden, another sinking feeling hits my fragile stomach, reason. I hate you so much, reason. The realities of earning income and getting experience settle in, right alongside the cocktail of vices and sadness. My language barrier comes to mind, I could never have a real job here. I'd be backpacking or living off Adan. Our love is way too fresh to go there. The timing doesn't line up.

"If you have chemistry, you only need one other thing. Timing. But timing's a bitch." I remember the day I heard that line. It's from my favorite TV show. I was barely paying attention to How I Met Your Mother, but it was playing in the background of my bedroom as I printed out that week's assignment for my reporting class. The words suddenly caught my attention and I stopped what I was doing. I couldn't rewind it, so I took the nearest pen and wrote it down right on the front of my assignment, which was a short paper I hoped would be my animal story. Everyone has an animal story to highlight their career, our reporting professor told us. Mine was about a pig called Betty I saw at a farmer's market that weekend.

I was still single at the time and just settling into my first apartment in college. I hadn't yet gone through my heart ache or met Adan. I held up the paper with the quote written in red across the top.

"Ain't that the truth," I said as I reprinted my assignment and tucked that sheet away in a big folder, I have with loose notes I use for creative writing.

***

Standing past the stations and lines of airport security, I see Adan arrive and run to the farthest point. He's trying to say goodbye. He had class at the same time as our flight and ran here as soon as he could. We'd just gone through security and I'm startled when my phone rings. It's a bold move made in desperation. He's a poor graduate student that definitely cannot afford international cell phone rates.

"Hey," I said while looking at him. I already felt like I was in a different world.

"I'm sorry I missed it," he said. His tall lanky body was waving at me all sweaty and exasperated from running. I couldn't go back. My sister and I would miss our flight if I do security all over again

"I can't believe you came," I was fighting back tears. "I love you."

"I love you," he says as he puts his hand down.

"*Pasen, por favor,*" a short man in a blue suit nudges us to the elevator to keep moving.

"I gotta go," I say.

"I know," he says, and I see him blow me a kiss and hang up.

I put away my phone and I do as I'm told. I keep moving forward.

***

3 months later

It was excruciating from the get-go. Our Skype call began with all the usual mushy nicknames which immediately made my face tighten.

"Hey bubblegum drops. How are you? You look pretty even blurry," he said. His dark-framed glasses and tiny bedroom visible from my Dell. The tiny bedroom I was just sleeping in and holding him in just a few short months ago. My luggage still smells like this room.

"Adan, I don't know how to say this," I start and immediately the words taste bad.

He knows. We always know.

"I thought this was coming," he puts his head down.

"We're so far. We're in a different time zone. Once my day is gone and we talk, I've already shared everything. You're going to be there for at least four years. I don't know how else to make this work realistically?"

These are superficial reasons, but they sound good. The truth is I can't move to Spain and I need someone to hold and touch and love right here. The truth is this is making my insides explode. The truth is if we met at a different time, we'd probably end our search right here. But I can't. I want more. The truth I want to say but won't come out is, I will never forget you Adan, because you taught me how to love. I never held back with you once. I haven't felt love like this since being a kid. I'm mad you're moving. You could have stayed. I'm angry we met each other when we did, but I'm grateful you helped me pick up the pieces of my very broken heart and put it back together. I had a blind fool's faith that the best was always coming for us. I hope it still is.

None of that comes out. Only goodbye. The ding signifying our Skype ended rings and as soon as I hear it, I sob.

I weep until my roommate finds me. That was yesterday. Today, I'm packing my things and going back home to move in with my parents. Fuck my life. Inching closer to actual adulthood is nothing like what I thought. I had a plan to be college sweethearts with my first love, engaged by my senior year. Kids follow soon after. Career on the up and up.

Now, I'm applying to Teach America, for which I am not a shoe-in. Apparently, I'm graduating during the Great Depression of our time. That's an actual quote from the news. So, I'm 100% single and jobless. I just broke up with the man that could be the love of my life and my parents are in my very tiny apartment.

"Teach America. What's that?" my Dad says as he's packing boxes.

"You want to be a teacher?" My mom is folding clothes and packing all the Parisian decor she had bought me and hung on the walls of my bedroom.

"It's a program that pays you to move into urban areas and help kids," I say.

Nothing is casual with my parents.

"So," my Dad pauses. "Let me get this right, to see if I understand. You are going to apply to a job that will pay you peanuts and send you to live in a crime-ridden neighborhood? So, you can teach? Is that right?"

"Sort of."

"Okay, do I have to be the one to say it? Are you out of your Goddamn mind?"

"Shhhh. You're not alone," Sofi comes in with more empty boxes. "People are going to hear you, Dad."

"Well, maybe they can help me talk your sister out of the idiotic story she just told me."

I roll my eyes. "Relax, Dad."

"I'm going to go pour myself a scotch," he puts down his boxes.

This is my Dad our entire life. I can't say I blame the guy. He had to grow up with three women. Our periods synced. We had breakups and drama and tantrums. Even our dog was a girl. And now, he's thinking of Dangerous Minds starring me: his firstborn child.

My mom is unphased. "Do we like this? I think it's outdated."

It's the one piece of clothing I bought for myself in the entire closet.

"We like that, yes."

My sister chimes in. "Mom, why don't I do the clothes?"

"I didn't say anything," my mother says, defensively packing my wardrobe. "It was just a question. Who else is going to be honest with you if it isn't me?"

"Excellent point," I go check my phone. I don't know what I'm hoping to find. It's too early in Spain and what the hell is Adan going to text anyway?

Sofi comes back, "Hey, you okay?"

"Yeah. It's just a lot. Seeing all my stuff in boxes. Going back home. This is home."

"Well, remember when you hated it here? Everything in life takes getting used to. You'll make it work back home. It's not so bad. You live in Miami, not some small town with nothing going on."

"I think that's all of it," I hear my mom yell.

They all go downstairs to the car and I remain in my empty apartment to lock it up one last time. My first apartment. The walls look bare except for a constellation of nails where our photos were hung up. I can see all my best memories here. A kitchen full of us pre-gaming, which never felt like having a few drinks to make the night cheaper but instead getting obliterated before it even began. The couches I would watch reality TV on with my roommate Arielle and her boyfriend while he smoked pot and I got a second-hand high. My bedroom where I've cried and laughed and loved and lost. I don't want to leave any of this to go back to my prepubescent bedroom at home. I don't even know that girl anymore.

3
A generation of G chat employees

"This is the first day of your new life."

I am actually saying this shit out loud to myself in front of the bathroom mirror at my first job.

"Today is going to be awesome. You look great."

Okay. We're done here.

It's Thursday. There's nothing particularly exciting about this Thursday, only that the following day is the last day until the weekend. The blobs of goo in my lava lamp fight each other into bubbly submission. Dollops create and recreate themselves, changing patterns and shapes.

"Cris, we need this by 11 AM. Can you do it?" My boss hands me a long list of publications to call and a press release about a has-been soccer player setting up an insurance-sponsored camp in a small local park.

I look up from the blobs slowly. "Sure."

There's no way in hell they're covering this. I'm not particularly hoping they pick up this BS story either. In fact, a small part of me roots for their journalistic integrity.

One by one, each publication gets a tailored version of the same email: Hi, Mrs. Garcia, I hope this note finds you well. I read this greeting a week into the job in a co-worker's email and I've been starting all my emails this way ever since. Six months to be exact. That's how long I've been working here, my first real job.

The fate of this story doesn't concern me. It should, but I'm a writer. I know what makes good writing. It doesn't happen often but sometimes when I'm feeling motivated, I'll actually call and follow up on my steaming pile of poop story. Today, my coffee was extra sweet, and I've got some time to kill. May as well.

"Hey, Cathy, how are you?"

"Great. What's up?"

"Just shot you a note about a feel-good feature that may be nice to include."

She tells me to hold as the sounds of clicking and scrolling follow her voice. "Ehhh. I'll letcha know if we run it."

I could have told my supervisor this would happen, but she wouldn't have listened to me anyway, so I repeat the motions that are asked of me. This is Miami, a growing city with all kinds of relevant news clamoring for attention. Not to mention we're in Florida, home of the Florida Man, and a state that's become known for the sheer volume of weird news we produce. Nobody cares that a once famous Mexican soccer player from L.A. will be giving children lessons at Tropical Park next Saturday at noon. Even less so that it's sponsored by an insurance company. Of course, this story got a real hard pass.

I work at an agency taking care of the Hispanic public relations for a big-name insurance company based on the West Coast, a coast that is worlds away from who we are on the East Coast. The Hispanics are different, the culture is different. To the insurance company, though, we're all the same. This ignorance is not something any of the Hispanic people in this office snub their nose at. They smile and win the business. Of course, we can speak to any Hispanic population! Most presentations to prospective clients begin with the same obvious explanation, it shouldn't be surprising to people, but it is: Hispanics are not all the same.

As Hispanics, we are the fastest growing minority— "soon to be majority"—as several demographic packets say. Last year's census dubbed Miami the "gateway to Latin America," and businesses here could not be happier.

Everyone is excited at what these studies mean—more money.

As I suspected, two Spanish language publications cover this story. But they're just web sites filled with streaming ads. This story will get lost among a hundred other re-printed press releases. I'm not even sure who's reading it.

"Only two? Really?" my supervisor is stupefied.

"Really. I can only call and follow up. I can't exactly make the story interesting. Would you print this?"

She scrunches up her face. Of course, she wouldn't, but she would have sold it. "*Bueno, gracias. ¿Por qué no hablamos luego?*" Well, thanks anyway. Let's talk later.

"Of course," I smile.

Like most second-generation Hispanic kids, I oversold my ability to navigate Spanish and really played up the bilingual aspect on my resume. I wouldn't have found a job here if I hadn't. My nearly perfect English accent doesn't shout Hispanic. In Miami, everyone's English has an accent, whether they also speak Spanish or not. It sounds like the letter "y" is aggressively shoved into every word.

Sí, como no, hablo español. This is the best sentence I can pronounce, and one I mastered for the interviewing process: "Yes, of course, I speak Spanish." Anything else is a struggle, but how much Spanish do they actually need me to speak on a job technically in America anyway?

Turns out, a lot.

Most of the staff speaks English except for the creative team, the people I need to communicate with the most. They came here from countries like Cuba, Venezuela and Colombia, and literally don't speak one word of English. People can—and do—live entire lives in Miami without learning English. Luckily, most of the creatives I work with want to learn English as much as I want to improve my Spanish, so our conversations entail broken Spanish (me) responding to broken English (them). One day at a time, we will both learn our way into actual bilingualism.

Post-census, everyone seems to be confused about who they are. I, for example, filled "other" for race, as my options were Native American, African American, Asian or White. Despite having a milky complexion, I have been reminded many times in life how not white I am. *Where are you really from?* was always a follow up question for me in college. Even so, my dad was happy it was me that went away (versus my sister who has a brown complexion just like his) because I could blend in better (and be safer). There were moments growing up my parents didn't feel safe enough to stop in certain places because of how they looked. I am the family snowflake, so I felt in a move of solidarity, I would be "other" as well.

Surprisingly, this horrified both my parents who expressly told me we are 100% white.

Weeks ago, during one of my mandated Sunday family days, the conversation regarding our race and ethnicity came up.

"Okay, but what about Hispanic?" I asked. "Wouldn't that be more appropriate?"

"We aren't Hispanic." They stared at me blankly and as if I just accused them of a crime.

"Oh, no?"

"We're European," my mother said in her Spanish accent.

"Mom, we're Hispanic. The word is inclusive of all people who speak Spanish, i.e. us."

"Yes, Spain is in Europe. Hispanics are South American."

A common misconception.

"What if we're Italian?" my Dad chimes in.

"Dad. We are not Italian."

My parents were born in Cuba, but their family lineage originated in Spain. When Cuba fell to communism, my mother moved back to Spain and my father moved to the United States. But all of that doesn't matter, they grew up in a different generation of Hispanics who did not want to stand out because that was dangerous. To be the same meant acceptance, success, safety.

When my dad was a child growing up in Central Florida, he was teased for being Hispanic on account that he looked the part. When he was 17, he was stopped on the side of the road by cops who threw him onto the hood of his car and shoved a pistol to the back of his neck. He was simply driving when two cop cars pulled him over and demanded he get out of the car. It was standard protocol, they said, he looked like "a Mexican who shot a cop nearby."

So, I understand where they're coming from, but it doesn't change the fact that we are definitely Hispanic. Our conversation alone gives us away. Hispanic conversations always look angry because we speak over each other and much louder than necessary. Were we white, I'd probably be more concerned if our neighbors could hear us. They definitely could.

Five separate Google searches later, we confirmed we are in fact Hispanic and can be considered racially white. According to the 2006 U.S. census, Hispanic is not a race but an ethnicity, or a cultural identification, and in some cases a choice depending on what you personally identify with. Meaning in America, my parents can technically be white Italians.

Back at work, I suppress the questions regarding my identity and press on.

"Good morning!" the HR woman says to me as she walks in and passes my cubicle. I smile tartly in response.

On Gchat, I confer with several other bored friends with full time jobs.

Is it ridiculous that I'm annoyed at the HR woman for coming in every morning and saying "Good Morning" like it's some kind of surprise we're all still here?

I think you're being a bit harsh but I'm listening.

I'm here every morning at the same time. WHY does this feel like Groundhog Day?

Oh, Ms. QLC. So it goes... Good morning btw.

Morning haha

Ms. QLC— short for Quarter Life Crisis. I earned the nickname these past few months working through what at first felt like a depression but I'm now starting to realize is a scary realization that the "real world" feels like a bait and switch. When I graduated from college, I had a purpose. The world was filled with possibility, I can still recall back to that feeling of butterflies that I could make a difference. Every day I strain a little more to feel it. It's fading quickly.

Advertising agencies are tricky too. There's a strange allure to working in a building decorated like a playground. It's purposefully constructed to fool you. Every agency I interviewed at had all types of fun office décor, like giant bean bags that implied "we're so not corporate," toys in every corner, modern art because "sure, we sell things, but we're all really artists," and my favorite, the graphic T-shirt and converse-only uniform. I bought the story these shiny objects sold. When I got here though, it was different. It does have its fun compared to working at, let's say Carmax, but it's a cutthroat environment. This is a business like any other, worse even, because no one's job is guaranteed. Our salaries don't come from the company, they come from our client. Lose a client, lose your job. During my six months here, I've seen an entire team go in a day. Their client decided they wanted a change in creative direction and just like that 20 people were gone. That uncertainty is hard to get used to but I don't mind it as much as the long hours we're all expected to log in happily on our bean bags.

A man in a small metal scooter whizzes by my desk. He's pedaling in the hall to his office and the other newbies look with awe. Man, this is such a cool place, one girl says. Sure, you can wheel your ass from one corner of the office to the other but don't even think about walking outside.

Damn. It's still only 10:22 AM. I have seven hours and thirty-eight more minutes to go. I check back in with my friend.

Had to do some pitching this morning.

Any luck?

None whatsoever. What are you doing?

I'm filing paperwork. It'll probably take me 15 minutes, but I'll send it in two hours. God I hate having to justify an 8-hour workday.

You and me both.

The problem is the grind. This work system is flawed, and I'm surprised more people from the generation before us don't see it. Months ago, I was the leave-it-to beaver newbie. I raised my hand first. I did the homework and extra credit. I had moxie. But after putting in all that effort, I realized I was simply the fastest hamster running in its wheel. We are not paid to work forty hours, we are paid to be present that long. It's an important distinction and one that took me some time to figure out. Having us sit in a chair in an office, under their supervision, makes the boss feel better.

But I need a paycheck to pay the rent. That puppet from Team America World Police was right, freedom isn't free. At 2 pm, I know I can comfortably go home, but I will wait, read horoscopes, watch YouTube videos and Gchat other indentured servants going through the same process.

I'm stuck here because I don't think it's different anywhere else. I don't know where to go. I wish I felt the same genuine excitement as I did in college. When I walked through the campus and could feel the possibilities. I've never felt that kind of palpable curiosity anywhere else. Maybe I should go back to school. What the hell would I do?

Back in college, the counselors at the University of Florida told me they like grad school candidates that have work experience. I don't want to get a Masters in Communications. That seems useless. Maybe an MFA in Creative Writing, but I'm not a real writer. I mean, sure, I've written my whole life but it's probably not any good. I only had one professor tell me I was the least bit talented and it was in high school for a short horror story. I still remember the day. It took me by surprise.

Everyone was in class; the cool, outgoing kids were talking to the teacher as I, a shy teenager, sat alone in the back texting my boyfriend who went to another school. A few moments later as class began, I heard the teacher call my name. I was shocked to hear it come out of his mouth. I honestly thought he may not even know who I was. In fact, a little part of me felt my getting up when he called my name was a surprise verification of my identity. I imagined him reading my story to his utter amusement and then checking who this delightful author was, only to be like, Cris... Cris?

He announced my short story was the best in class and he handed me my paper with his notes. It was the first time I ever felt acknowledged for some sort of talent, like maybe I could be a writer if I wanted to.

Most graduate programs require writing samples. I could turn in this book I've started. There's plenty of material there. At least some of it should prove I have a talent that can be molded. What are they going to think about my major though? Public Relations immediately puts me into such a stereotype, especially since I'm a woman. What if they Facebook me? Then they'll see I'm blonde. Blonde PR girl does not denote a serious artist.

Well, what if they don't? Shouldn't it be about the writing? My writing is good. It can be worked with. Maybe my unexpected background and appearance will show dedication to a true calling in the arts yet an understanding of the mainstream. I can leave my job to pursue financial debt and a writing career. I have the heart of a starving artist.

***

Delighted with my newfound identity, I become drunk with power and more brazen in my slacking at work. These people don't get it. They're all part of the machine. I decide it's better not to corrupt my personal morals so cutting out of work early becomes a regular part of my routine. Usually, I meet my friends at a happy hour nearby to complain about my job and then spend most of my earnings on expensive cocktails.

Happy hour is a new phenomenon to me. In college, drinking was cheap and accessible at any time, but in the adult world people wait until 6 PM and then rush to go have a drink— unless they are awake to their oppression and duck out early like me. I'm meeting Cassandra, who works at a hospital nearby as a children's therapist.

"Hello, my friend," we kiss each other on the cheek, the customary greeting in Miami.

"Hi love. How was your day?" I slide a vodka tonic towards her. Our usual drink for the moment. We go through phases.

She sips it and pauses to close her eyes. "Long." Her dark complexion and brown hair paired with big caramel eyes reveal a Colombian-Cuban heritage. Her features are exaggerated and beautiful, like a doll. They're the shades I've envied my entire life growing up surrounded by exotic beauties. I quite literally pale in comparison with my milky skin, naturally black hair currently highlighted blonde and green eyes— my one redeeming quality. The blonde adds some sort of differentiating factor.

"Same."

The music is too loud, but we come anyway. It's convenient and there are plenty of single men who make their way here. We rarely ever meet anyone once we get into our long, intense conversations though.

"I wish I didn't think so much," I say.

"I think it's a good thing to think so much. You should embrace your deep thinking."

"I guess, but I'm not sure how productive it is," I take a long sip. "I always end up unsatisfied and feeling guilty. I just have a feeling the things that really matter in life are not what I'm doing. And I hate having to participate in this system because that's the way it is. I spend most of my day on Gchat, legitimately. Oh, and I need to move out of my parent's house, like, tomorrow."

I can't help but think our baby faces are more pronounced in the sleek blazers we're wearing. Do we look like kids playing dress up? Sometimes I feel like that's the case.

"It's true. I know. Sometimes I'm not sure if what I do is making a difference. Mental health is so complicated," she takes a sip. "I mean, am I even helping? Sometimes I don't know."

And now comes my guilt. "At least you're doing something that really matters," I put my hand on her shoulder. "What's more important than trying to help each other? I sell shit people don't need and waste a lot of time."

She laughs. "There's a purpose to everything. You've just gotta find it. Maybe it's not at this job but there's something there that'll lead you to that next step. I sure hope that's the case for me."

"I wish I could turn it around. I feel so negative and I know we're so blessed compared to the rest of the world. But honestly, all I can see is what isn't working... take happy hour right now. Is it crazy I think even being here at happy hour is somehow participating in the cookie cutter process? Like, they steal your day by making you sit in a small desk and it makes it to the point where you need to leave and grab a drink. And, oh, how convenient they build bars with over-priced specials right around the corner."

We laugh.

"Well maybe we can't escape it," she says. "Maybe we're fucked in the system."

I raise my glass to hers and they make a light clink noise. "To a generation of Gchat employees."

4
Katy Perry, a nun and Julia Roberts walk into a bar

Florence and the Machine blares over the speakers, the smell of hairspray and conditioner fills the room, and two of my girlfriends walk around in their bras and underskirt tutus. It's Halloween night in Miami and we are twenty-four. Our toned bodies are canvases of glitter and desire. We sip Jack Daniels and Ginger Ale, taking breaks only to gloss our lips, widen our cat eyes and gently stroke our cheeks with bronzer, giving our baby fat a more aggressive bone structure.

Butterflies of anticipation and nerves rush through our bodies, the alcohol no doubt contributing. There's nothing in this world like feeling young and beautiful. I drink in the moment, because confidence rarely makes its way through. I've never felt beautiful. I've always been cute. In fact, I loathe the word cute and it's condescending tartness.

She's so cute. Never beautiful. Never sexy. Just, you know, cute.

Maybe it's the alcohol or our commitment to making Halloween epic, but today I feel sexy. Four dark angels stand in front of the mirror, a purposeful choice. Our matching black halos and leotards are slimming. I suck in my belly and pose in front of the mirror from a few different angles. Not bad. The tutu hides the little pooch below my navel I've come to despise ever since low-cut Brazilian jeans became a thing.

"You guys ready?" Celeste asks, she is punching our destination into her maps.

"Just about," I smooth out my belly area and take a gulp of my drink. The ice melted and it goes down cold.

"We look a-m-a-z-i-n-g," my sister drags out the word. "Like, OMG we're gonna get into some trouble tonight."

"I hope so," Cassandra says. "You ready?"

"Let's do it." I say finishing the last of my drink.

All four of us pile into Cassandra's black BMW. She is always the designated driver. The trip goes by fast. We are floating. The promise and potential of the night are on our minds, I can tell. Everyone goes out on Halloween and it's making us even more intoxicated. The music in the car is as loud as our anticipation is high, we travel down the long Miami expressway passing palm trees, buildings, billboards and lights.

Our destination is a giant Miami Beach home. The gaudy structure was converted into a magnificent lounge where past bedrooms and living rooms now serve as themed bars. The whole of it looks like a real house party, a relic from the 90's movies that glorified the genre. We pull up getting just the right spot. Already a good sign.

We begin the only place we know where: the first bar we see. The telltale signs for spotting the bar is easy, plenty of people crowding a small space. Bars are like the kitchens in houses, everyone congregates there no matter how much free room you give them. This one looks to be exactly where the kitchen was when someone used to live here. Now, it's a neon bar with doctors, angels, cats and Harry Potter gathered around sipping cocktails and making conversation.

"Four whiskey gingers?" Celeste asks, raising four fingers as she makes her way to the bar.

"Yes, please!" we all shout hanging close enough to grab drinks as they come.

"Wow, this place is unlike anything I've ever seen," I say to Cassandra practically yelling. The music is so loud our conversations are short sentences screamed and with lots of hand gestures.

Cassandra nods at me exaggeratedly, "Yes!"

A cold whiskey ginger touches my arm and I begin to pass them back. There. We're all armed with our social lubricant. A little bit of that helps us as we slip through the miasma of sticky limbs making it to our desired point in the mansion. Once I'm buzzed, the crowded, sweaty bodies we shimmy between are enticing, even poetic. I get so close to some people I can smell their aftershave and hear brief but telling snippets of their conversation. *And then she never called me back. Can you believe that, bro?* No matter the subject, the intention is always the same. We're here for one purpose and that's to connect. I remind myself of this when I get nervous or self-conscious in large crowds. Some people want to connect physically, others want to be seen and flattered. We are all searching for validation and that puts us all on an equal playing field.

We find a little nook by a room that looks like a library, except there's a DJ playing some kind of nondescript hip hop. It sounds like underground music, the type of music you only have access to by being in places like this. Blue and yellow lights from the DJ booth twist into geometric shapes and our dancing bodies are the backdrop for them.

I'm not sure which I want. I take a sip of my drink and smear off sweat from my bicep. We're laughing and linking arms dancing and for a brief moment I feel free. And then I catch strangers making subtle eye contact with their intended targets. I suddenly feel like fresh meat.

F. Scott Fitzgerald's familiar words from The Great Gatsby enter my mind: "He gives large parties and I like large parties.

They're so intimate. There isn't any privacy at small parties." It's a truth I've known my entire life as a wallflower. It's so easy to blend into the pulse of a large party and take the time to scope out the attention of the only person I really want to spend the night with. We all evolve with time, that's true, but the core of us does not change. Even now with the most confidence I've had in a while, I am looking for the exit sign.

As the girls find some old friends from college I don't quite recognize, I take my chance and escape for my first break, greeted with the light breeze that marks Miami's spring-like October. While the world is bundling up for fall, I get to dress in a leotard without feeling the slightest chill. No wonder real estate here is astronomical. This place must be worth a fortune.

Leaning against a Liberace-like fountain, I can't help but wish I smoked. If only my hands could stay busy, then I wouldn't need to grab my phone. The glare of my halo projects a silver light onto the screen. For the briefest of seconds, I can see my reflection. It's the curious details that imprint themselves in our memory. Right now, I feel the image of my 24-year-old eyes, nose and mouth embedding itself into my mind. I've always been a nostalgic person, calling upon the past and even the future's past in many of life's present moments. It's a trait I've tried to remedy since I was young.

The phone unlocks, revealing a text message. It's a boy.

There's always a boy. For me, anyway.

The casualness of early twenties dating is a game you can win if you really want to play. But my sensitivity has never made it seem winnable. A part of me wants to own being alone tonight, to resist the urge to check the message and even more the desire to respond. Another part of me cannot help feeling the craving to be wanted. I search to fill that need as much as I participate in the game. Somehow though, no matter how in control I feel when I'm playing it, somewhere along the way I find myself feeling like I'm losing.

How are you?

A simple message, but he cares. Or does he? Resentment builds up in my shoulders. I hate that I feel relieved he checked in. I put the phone away feeling somehow more victorious for not answering. My itchy costume rides up intimate crevices and I suddenly don't feel sexy anymore. I need another drink.

Back inside, the night takes a turn without prior notice or permission. I see my sister walking over with Celeste holding her by the wrist like a child.

"Cristina," she says impatiently using my full name, never a good sign. "We need to talk to Vincent. His girlfriend told off Celeste and insulted her."

"Is this true?" Celeste nods somewhat embarrassed.

Jealous lovers are never a good idea to mix with cocktails. The once alluring crowd is now oversaturated with rude, unaware drunks and my shoulders sink back in resignation. "Alright, sure."

Before I can understand the full scope of whatever shit just went down, I am watching my sister find Vincent and explain to him excitedly what happened as Celeste stands there like a toddler whose mother is complaining to the principal. This is Celeste though, always the passenger, never the driver. Her inability to navigate her own life effectively has always made me want to protect her. It's an inclination I know the origin of quite well.

When I was a toddler my mother was pushing me through the mall in my stroller. All of a sudden, another mom pushing her toddler in a stroller passed us and her small child smacked me across the face. I did nothing. I sat there dumbfounded. I didn't even cry. When my mom told me this story in my teenage years, a disgust filled my stomach at how utterly pathetic I was. Who gets slapped and just sits there? Never mind that I was a child whose innocence did not yet know the tidal wave of bullshit life entails. Never mind that it isn't exactly rational to judge my tiny two-year-old self for not yet knowing what a dickhead was. It was too late, the story eradicated any tolerance in my life for bullying or defenselessness.

This is the same defenselessness I see in Celeste. It makes me want to go and say her peace for her (as Sofi is now doing), however unhealthy it is. As I see my sister doing this though, while Celeste idly sits by, it makes me think. Should we really be doing this? Maybe Celeste needs a good slap in the face.

I want to impart this newfound wisdom to my sister, but before I can, I see Vincent raise his arms up. I imagine he is saying calming words like, I'll take care of it or This is all a misunderstanding, I'm sure of it.

I don't want this problem to be ours, and yet somehow, I've just let it be.

"Let's go to the bathroom," I say and I grab my sister and lead her to a quiet place. Perhaps, I can talk to her so we can transfer this drama back to its rightful owner.

However, Mother Nature is a force to be reckoned with. Sometimes, you want the night to go one way and instead you find yourself in the midst of a verbal bathroom brawl led by a petite young woman dressed like a nun. Such is the situation we've just created.

"Did you talk to my fucking boyfriend?" the nun shrieks at my sister, her voice echoing off the bathroom mirrors.

"Who the hell are you?" my sister responds, genuinely confused.

"I'm Vincent's fucking girlfriend. You know, the guy you just told some made-up bullshit about. I didn't call anyone a slut and you're a goddamn liar." She points at my sister as she adjusts her black and white tunic.

My sister's chest rises with the breath of someone who is getting ready to clap back. And this makes me very nervous. Because I know my sister, and she will show this aggravated nun just what crazy in a bathroom at a club in Miami can be when you yell at the wrong person.

And so, with all the strength I have ever mustered in my life, I pluck her tiny body from the nun's clutches and maneuver her around the crowd of other costumed girls who don't care about our problem and just want to pee. It's not the first cat fight they've seen in a restroom.

Before I can even ask what the hell that was about, my sister finds Vincent yet again, only this time she is not so excited, she is yelling over the music as his eyes widen like a deer in headlights.

Apparently, during my non-smoking smoke break, a drunken misunderstanding transpired as Celeste was flirtatiously dancing with Vincent. A California Girl Katy Perry—an important distinction to note as there are several Katy Perrys floating around the mansion—pulled her aside and schooled her on the type of behavior that is acceptable with men when they have girlfriends. That illuminating clarification ended with Celeste being called a slut, in so many words. We assumed that was Vincent's girlfriend. We came to find out she was not.

When my sister told Vincent that his crazy girlfriend should back off, he dutifully relayed this message to his girlfriend (the nun). Alas, our reverent sister did not take the role of alleged perpetrator lightly.

As the nun comes stampeding out of the bathroom making a bee line for my sister and Vincent, I grab my sister once again, fighting through the crowd of famous movie characters in the hallway. I begin losing hope as the nun inches closer, but then a miracle appears. A kind soul opens a passageway for us right in the nick of time.

As I raise my head to mouth the words Thank you to our guardian angel, I come face-to-face with California Girl Katy Perry. She pats me on my shoulder, "No problem, girl. It's a nightmare here tonight." Then she wisps away, heading straight to the shit show we abandoned.

"Was that?" I look at my sister.

"There's no time."

We find Cassandra bumming a smoke in the front lawn and signal to her it's time to go. We walk quickly to the car and pile into it like it's a getaway van. Cassandra grabs the wheel and checks her mascara blissfully unaware of our impatience to get out. "Where to?"

"Let's try another party," I say. "What are the options?"

Celeste checks her phone and sends a few texts. "We can try this other spot. I know a few people there."

"Fuck it," I say. Wasting a killer outfit is a sin in your twenties.

This next bar is a short drive away. It's not my favorite to say the least. It's the kind of bar that makes me constantly tired. It's always playing slow music and there's never enough going on, but I'll take what we can get at this time of night. We arrive outside and proceed to circle the parking lot three times.

"I don't believe this," Cassandra says waving her arms. This is not a good sign for two reasons.

First, if we go any further, we will park in a no-good-very-bad area of town that four dark angels should never, ever feel safe parking in. Second, Cassandra has an airy expectation for good things to happen in life that is always met by success, and among those things is parking. She has the parking karma of someone who must have died in a horrific accident. Come hell or high water, the universe always delivers her a spot— and usually a good one. It's uncanny her ability to see a jungle of cars and say without hesitation we are finding a VIP spot, and then miraculously, a car pulls out right before her. Always. In fact, this is part of the reason she usually drives. If Cassandra cannot find a spot, a spot doesn't exist.

Out of dog-headedness we don't give up—it's a stubborn quality of our youth. In a final act of defiance to the night, we drive to one last club, also nearby.

"Okay, we can try this new place by Wynwood," Celeste says. She's always good at finding a back-up plan.

"Oh no," Cassandra gasps.

"What?" we all three say in unison.

"I need a bathroom."

We pull into the nearest Denny's and walk in without acknowledging the hostess. She doesn't seem to care. Usually, I would at least pretend like we're planning to order something, but there are urgent matters at hand. This is an emergency.

Inside the dirty stall, Cassandra shrieks.

"Noo!"

"What?!"

"I have my period. I don't have anything, not one tampon or pad."

We each do a quick scan of our tiny purses, but who are we kidding, we can barely fit gum in there. We don't have a thing.

Cassandra begins to giggle. It's a nervous angsty giggle and it's contagious. One by one we all start to laugh so hard we're crying, and our faces are frozen in that ugly way that means we're really laughing from our gut. It's over. Our night does not survive the spontaneous period.

Four dejected angels return to home base, a large intricate house belonging to Cassandra's mom. The residence has its own personality. I call it The House on Malaga, an ode to The House on Mango Street. I remember vividly a chapter where its young protagonist drives through a nice neighborhood, imagining one day she'd get to live there. This neighborhood was that one for me as a child. I'd drive down one of its wide streets staring at the large houses and trees lining its road with hanging moss. I felt like that little girl in the book.

And now this house, located on Malaga Street, has significance to me. It's not a desire to live here anymore per se, though it is coincidental a house so special to me would be on this street. The House on Malaga is more than Cassandra's house. To simply dismiss it as a dwelling, as so many of us do to the structures that house us for years, would be short-sighted. This home has seen more things, absorbed more tears and bore witness to the moments that have defined our young adulthood thus far. It is our final resting point on this All Hallows Eve, the inevitable end the night has been persuasively leading us to.

I look in the mirror one final time before removing my costume, makeup and enthusiasm. It's time to surrender. It's time to sit around the TV and watch My Best Friend's Wedding while snacking on comfort food. I grab my phone, getting ready to finally respond to the text message, when something disturbing catches my ear.

"She's how old?" I ask.

"Twenty-fucking-two!" Cassandra answers with shocking disdain. It's the scene when Cameron Diaz, Kimmy, says she's dropping out of college for her fiancé.

"Wow, were we asleep when we saw this?" I say putting down the bag of trail mix, a pathetic midnight snack for which the girls always make fun of me. Eat McDonald's like a real woman, my sister often says.

When I originally saw this film, a pitifully defeated Julia Roberts, Julianne, failed to break up her former lover's engagement. I always felt sorry for her that she lost the man of her dreams to the younger blonde Kimmy. I realize now how frightfully wrong I was. Julianne was the true victor all along.

"Holy shit," I said. A handful of nuts crunching loudly in my head.

"Holy shit is right," says Cassandra. "That is fucked up."

I know I'm doing that thing again, living in the future's past, but I can't help but feel in my bones this is a sign. Something is clicking. I put the phone away for a final time, never responding again to the boy. Because, well, he's a boy, immature and playing an obvious game. A weak game. And instead of raising my standards and elevating the playing field, I've been meeting him at his.

I've been stuck between the same two opposing desires that have motivated my life since college: wanting to be loved, to get the guy, and wanting to be independent, to live my life.

It's always seemed like an either-or choice. I either fall in love or go out and live an interesting life alone. Instead, I've been creating a half-ass version of both, going out to bars and searching for love, never present or committed to one way of being.

Maybe I've been trying to be Kimmy when this entire time I've been Julianne.

5

That time I went to a psychic

I get in Cassandra's car not knowing what exactly I'll be walking into.

"She's great. Honestly, all my friends go to her. She's like a sweet grandma," Cassandra says, gripping the wheel and driving us deep into the suburbs.

"Jesus, this is really out West," I say. Butterflies fill my stomach. I'm excited.

"We're about ten minutes out." She smiles.

We're on our way to a tarot card reader. I've never been to one, but I will pay any price to bypass the pain stemming from my uncertainty. This Cuban grandmother in suburbia is my hope, my life-hack to confirming if I will get my shit together and live happily ever after.

It's scary, but I need this. My MFA applications have become a mountain of anxiety and debt. I've spent $1,500, which is a lot for me. About half a month's salary to be exact.

In a twist of irony, the miserable soul-sucking job I once loathed has turned from tolerable to enjoyable. Since I've stopped defining myself as an advertising slave in favor of my true identity—a struggling writer and future grad student—the same mundane tasks have taken on a different purpose. I'm working towards a bigger artistic vision. My job turned into a "day job," and just like that, I sort of like it.

"This is it."

The home is exactly as I'd pictured it would be. Cassandra leads me inside. A little old woman with puffy blonde hair and bright pink lipstick opens the door. She looks like a Golden Girl, the type of woman that makes you feel taken care of.

Cassandra elects to go first. This leaves me to wait in a small closed-off living room. The lady smiles and turns on the television.

"You can read a magazine or watch TV," she says and gently slides the doors closed. I can hear murmurs and laughter. They're having fun. She's a sweet grandmother who would never tell us anything bad.

I look at the TV, but it makes no difference. I don't even register what's on. My body is trembling. I begin to laugh at myself. It feels ridiculous to look down at my thighs and see the tremors come; my teeth are even chattering.

I pull out my phone, but I find little comfort there. Text messages from friends and guys I don't care enough about, pictures from happier drunk times, a few unanswered emails which don't matter enough to address on a Saturday. I don't have anything to distract myself with. What if she tells me I'm going to be alone forever? That I'm destined to have loved twice in my life, both instances behind me. What if I won't ever have kids? I don't know if I even want kids. You never do unless you think you can't.

And then suddenly I'm back in another time my legs shook convulsively. I was in a doctor's office, a fertility specialist. It was the fourth doctor I had to go see because my period spontaneously left me. It had been eight months, and I wasn't pregnant. Some doctors were less concerned. You technically don't need it, my gynecologist said. But if you want a period, I can give you birth control.

No thanks, I responded. And so instead, I opted to visit several specialists, hoping someone could make me bleed again one day.

The last stop was a fertility doctor. He looked at my blood work and asked me a few very personal questions. I went alone. It felt like it was the adult thing to do. He told me everything was clear as far as serious problems, like cancer or STDs. I'm probably really stressed, and these things happen. It's fine, but I may have difficulty having children one day.

Everything he said was white noise after that. You know those scenes in movies when you get bad news and the room disappears? That's exactly how it felt. He had to wave his hands to make sure I was with him. I nodded yes. I was nineteen. I didn't even have a boyfriend, but the thought that I'd have difficulty having kids was like having a dream I never knew I wanted taken away from me violently. I cried and wanted to forget. Months later my period came back and erased the whole incident.

It's a funny thing trying to forget about things only to be reminded of them at the most seemingly mundane times. One day at work not so long ago, I was in the stall waiting to pee. Another coworker was there too, in the stall next to mine, also trying to pee. There was a long pause as I willed my bladder to release. Finally we both peed but when we were washing our hands she turned to me and said, "Don't you hate when it takes a while to start?"

It's not like we both weren't thinking about it. "Yeah," I said awkwardly.

"It happens. Gets worse when you're older. Means you might have trouble having kids." She rolled up some paper, threw it in the bin and walked out.

It was so abrupt the way she said it. All I could do was look in the mirror like a loaded gun was staring back at me. There I was, my pretty but bloated face, my arms that were slightly too pudgy, my belly that was not flat enough but decent. Could be better, I shrugged. Except this time, I lingered. You better get your ass into shape. This kid thing could be a deal breaker someday.

And that was it. That was the last time I thought about the maybe very scary problem until right this very moment in a waiting room at a tarot card reader's house.

The doors open and startle me. It's Cassandra, smiling. "Your turn."

I sit at the table as the Golden Girl reshuffles her cards. Her light eyes stare at me through her thin-rimmed glasses. I can't be sure because I don't want to stare, but I think she has sparkly eyeshadow on.

"Hi, Mimi," she says and hands me the deck. It's an affectionate Spanish term you'd use with a granddaughter. "Go ahead and shuffle for a while. It still has your friend's energy on it."

"Of course." I shuffle and shuffle realizing immediately how much I suck at shuffling. I split the cards as I'm told, three piles.

"Pick one," she says, smiling expectantly.

"That one." I point to the middle stack. It's the biggest one so I figure I'll get more. Though I'm not sure that's how this works; it's not Buy-One-Get-One.

She begins to arrange the cards from all three piles. She studies them, looks up at me and then giggles.

"You were a curious little girl, weren't you?"

"What do you mean?"

She points her fat little finger at one of the cards as if she's referring to a memory plucked from my childhood and obviously laid bare on the table before us. All I see is a faceless woman in a field of flowers.

"I see you watching an old TV show. There's a skeleton. It's scary for a kid, but you want to see it anyway. You wait until it pops up, then you cover your eyes and run down the hall."

I know this memory. When I was young, my mom would let me watch the first few minutes of Tales of the Crypt. I loved scary movies, but I was too little to see them without getting nightmares, so my mom only let me see the beginning of this particular TV show. Every night I'd wait, see the intro and then cover my eyes and run when the skeleton showed up.

"How do you see that?" I said without hiding my genuine shock.

"Let's see what else I see." She looks back down and studies the cards. I can only see symbols I'm trying to judge. They seem neutral at the moment. Fields, flowers, stars and spheres.

"You're still that fearful little girl in many ways," she says, not looking up. "Why are you so scared of dying?" Now she looks directly into my eyes.

"I...I dunno. Dying is dying."

She shakes her head. "You're a very lucky girl, my dear. Very, very lucky. You've no reason to feel this much fear."

She flips over the cards to the next round and keeps studying them. "You are like your father." Her eyebrow arches. "Not much like your mother. She's a lot to handle. Your soul traveled with your father in another life."

"What about my sister?"

She flips some more and arches her eyebrow again. "Also difficult. You have a good family though. There's a lot of love there. You received a lot of love as a little girl. That's good. Who's the boy?"

"Which one?" There's always a boy.

"The one who hurt you," she looks back up. "Give me his birthday."

I blurt the date and she pens it down on her pad. There's a math equation she's doing though I can't quite make it out.

"Mmhmm," she keeps looking down. "Yes, he was bad. I don't like what I see. Very possessive, a lot of ego. A lot of anger." She emphasizes the last words in her broken English.

I nod in agreement. It's true, but it's not specific enough. She knows I want more.

"He hurt you. He still bares you ill will. His energy is strong and it affects you now. He's the reason you can't find a new love." She says his name. His whole name and now I'm really freaking out. She tells me his physical attributes, his blue eyes and walnut brown hair, right down to his broad shoulder blades. She sees him.

My chest gets hot with anger. Before she proved me right, I knew exactly who she was talking about. I believe in energy. I can feel his anger even now. Over the years, I've experienced it. I believe that if someone directs enough ill will your way it works, especially if you're still hooked. And even after all these years, he still has a hook in me, a direct line to my pain. I'm still not over the humiliation and scarring from our breakup.

"Well, that's not fair. What am I supposed to do with that?" I feel the indignation in my voice, but I can't help it. There doesn't seem to be much justice and I feel hopeless.

"No, no," she coos. "Don't worry, mi amor. This man, he is in for a lifetime of misery. I don't want that to comfort you, but you will move on. He won't get past his anger. He has a lot of hate in his heart. That will consume him. It will be a theme for the rest of his life. But his anger has nothing to do with you. It's his nature, it's his surroundings, it's beyond you. You're just caught in the middle of shared history. You need to cut this energetic cord. Te salvaste." She concludes. You saved yourself, the expression goes.

"Let go," she says. "It's in your holding on that gives it strength. Let go of what he did. He's different. You're different. You're trying to rewrite your past. It's already written. You cannot change the story. You cannot remove the ink. It's dry. All that's left for you to do is let go and forgive."

I wish I could forget about him, forget about the mess we made.

"Well, I was with him a long time ago. My recent ex, maybe try him."

"What's his birthday?"

"It's the same."

She laughs. "Okay then." She calculates the date, but this time flips another card. "Yes, I see. They're both similar except this one was much softer. Much better, much kinder. There is a lot of care here, but this is your past," she looks up at me to make sure I'm listening. "I know you want love. The answer will not be in looking back. This is all done." She moves the paper aside and keeps flipping cards. "I see three choices surrounding you now," she says.

"Options are good," I laugh nervously.

"Yes. One is a friend, but you don't like him. He's around. He calls you. You entertain him. He's not the one, but you can do it." She keeps flipping. "This second one is also a friend. Very ambitious, he'll be successful. You can do this too, though I still don't like him for you." She continues to flip until she pauses. "There. This one. Also, someone you know, not your type. You like those light eyes. But this one is the best one. I like him for you."

"Who is he?" I ask, searching my friends. I already know the first two she mentioned.

"He has olive skin, dark eyes and short dark hair. Not your type physically, but he is good. Un pedazo de pan." She drags the words; it's a Spanish phrase, a slice of bread. It means someone is kind, gentle, easy. "Choose him if you can. This is the best one. This will work. I like this for you a lot."

She keeps flipping, but I'm going through a bank of my friends. Olive skin, dark eyes, dark hair. I can't think of anyone. There's this guy I met a few weekends ago, maybe him? He's a relatively new friend. Fits the description, gorgeous.

She's already moved on.

"You have a good job," she states without question. "I see this building. I think I know this company."

I've no doubt. Miami is a small world. Here, I volunteer my information. I don't care about work. I want to know about the olive-skinned friend.

"Yes, you're doing well," she smiles proudly. "You're going

to rise up until you can't." Her nose scrunches.

"What do you mean?"

She shakes her head with a sad expression for me. "This company is going to go out of business. The leadership changed and there are bad deals that are starting. The milk is going sour."

Oh, no. Just last month the president of the company quit.

She shakes her head. "Don't worry you'll be fine. You have a lot of luck. You'll be successful in this."

"What about writing?" I ask too eagerly. My heart hurts a little that advertising is where she sees my success. "I'm leaving soon— for school I mean. Writing."

She looks confused. She doesn't see it so she keeps flipping to check her work. She scans the cards and then gets a little satisfied look. There it is. Thank God.

"You're not getting in," she says bluntly. Her satisfied look was for herself. She was content that she didn't miss it. This stings more than the friend I can't find.

"What? Really?" I say desperately.

"Yes, I'm sorry. One school will be between you and another man. They will debate, go back and forth; be prepared to send more material. But he's the better fit. They will choose him."

She sees my shoulders hunch down, the color drain from my face. This was the one thing I was sure about. I wasn't sure about my love life, but I sure as hell knew I'd be a starving MFA student.

"My dream is to write. Will I be a writer?"

She flips more cards. "Yes, you will. I think your money will come more from what you're doing now. You'll make a lot. But you will also be a writer."

I don't know what that means, but she smiles when she says it. She seems pleased for me.

"You've had a beautiful reading. Let go of some of that fear, my dear."

I walk out feeling the intangible promises of the future. I thought I'd feel the relief that comes from knowing what will happen. But all I feel is more uncertainty and frustration. Did I expect her to never mention my past? To give me a more concrete future? All I have are the same choices I had before coming in. I guess a part of me wanted her to do the work for me.

6

My first adult apartment

There comes a time in every girl's life when it's time to move into her first adult apartment. Although college is technically moving away, and that will always have been my first apartment, it isn't the same as a dwelling I choose and pay for. It isn't true independence, or at least it wasn't for me. Yes, I paid for my expenses, but my parents took care of my rent and books. There was a safety net. Today, that changes. It's the last time I'm waking up in my childhood bedroom and I could not be more thrilled. My parents on the other hand are less enthused.

"I still don't understand why you're moving. You're gonna waste a lot of money when you can stay here and save," my dad says rushing past me in our hallway talking over his shoulder. He's always in a hurry to do something.

"Good morning," I say, making my way to the guest bathroom, the one I've shared with my sister since we were children.

My eyes look tired, but they are twinkling. I am so excited; I can barely contain the smile that forms at the edges of my mouth. Today, I am free. As a matter of fact, I'm so delighted by my forthcoming move that I see all the things that used to aggravate me with a sense of appreciation, with graduation goggles as it's been referred to. The same rose-colored filter with which you see your senior year of high school is working for me. It shades out all the tumult and highlights only the good moments.

My parent's house, the house I grew up in, is in the suburbs. It's far too West of everything cool and relevant in Miami, at least for my stage in life. This is the area you move to when you're ready to settle down, tucked safely outside the city's action. But I ache to feel its pulse. I want to be in the fabric of what's happening, the busy streets lined with people speaking different languages, I want to be near the festivals and cultural events happening at the center of what is becoming a mecca of the art world, but more than any of that, I want to wake up in a place that is mine, all mine.

I make my way to get my first cup of coffee. It's a time I crave peaceful solitude. Since moving back in with my parents, it's nearly impossible to have a private coffee moment. Sometimes I'd sneak it into my room offering polite conversation on the way, though my entire body is pointing out the door and it's clear I don't want to engage. But today, I think, why not. I'll have the rest of my mornings all to myself. What's one more?

The bright sunshine and swaying tropical plants can be seen outside every window of my parent's house. They've turned it into a little oasis in an unexpected part of Miami.

"Pack your boxes, Cristina," my mom says. She's also talking to me over her shoulder as she passes through the kitchen. My mom is always up for a conversation, so I can tell she is feigning busyness.

I ignore her order, especially given that it's the first thing she's said to me today, because I know she is sad that I'm leaving. She feels like she's to blame. I tried to tell her that it wasn't about her, but she knows better. I cannot live with my mother. I cannot live with my parents, period, because it's time, but I really cannot live with my mother. Our personalities butt heads and in the last few years it's become difficult to hold a conversation without erupting in an all-out screaming match... and I'm not a yeller.

"Sure, Mom," I say and head to the living room to enjoy my coffee before taking my belongings out of this house where they shall never live again.

I take my first sip. This coffee reminds me of my parents, it's the taste of many mornings spent here. A bitter and sweet mixture of flavors but it's good enough with coconut milk. All the mugs here are eclectic and with no sense of coordination, much like what mine will be for now. I can tell they've bought their mugs in thrift stores and accumulated some from vacations we've taken, a mixture of their life before us and with us. I recognize the objects of our shared experience among the variety of others. The large cup with a moose that I'm currently sipping my coffee from is my favorite. I think I'll take this one with me. With loving detachment, I can see all the things I inherited from my parents... and our glaring differences.

I know I'm doing it again, experiencing a future nostalgia in the present moment, drinking in the scene of this home as its inhabitant for a final time. The dishes piled up every morning in the sink are overflowing today as usual, the three small bowls are placed underneath the kitchen island dedicated to each pet, two cats, one bossy and the other mellow and with a clear case of cat PTSD. The poor thing ate her own hair for the first 4 years of her life effectively giving herself a mohawk. My dad could often be heard greeting her in the mornings. *Hello Clarice*, he'd say in a creepily affectionate voice. What more could we expect from her with that name? The final bowl is for my sister's dog, who is fed first but still wants to eat the cat food.

I take another sip and my coffee is getting cold, so I head back in the kitchen to microwave it. They insist on brewing Dunkin' Donuts coffee even though they were my first advertising client, the same one that dropped our agency. Despite my constant reminders that their consumption reeks of betrayal, they continue to buy it in bulk.

I notice a recent addition in my kitchen. My mother bought a shelf for the wall with three spaces to hang mugs, each with a little chalkboard label: Dad, Mom and Sofi. No spot for me. I don't take it personally. In fact, it's kind of funny to notice the lengths of my mother's spite. I will miss her tiny acts of pettiness.

I'll miss the view of our driveway from the kitchen sink. There used to be a bench on the big tree in our front yard you can see right from this spot, my sister and I would swing on it when we were little. I remember seeing our extremely tall neighbor from this view too. As a kid, I would crawl on the counter and when I saw him coming, I'd yell for my dad. Our neighbor was a former cop and looked like one, always wearing a nondescript polo, shorts and Ray-Bans. He acted like he was on duty though he was retired, often coming over to inform my parents of the goings on in the neighborhood.

I'll miss all the plants my dad meticulously chose and planted in our front and back yards. All the different colors, textures and species that make our house look like a vacation rental. Their arrangement more than anything is a true testament of who my dad is, a gentle and disorganized nurturer. He put it all together and none of us understand (or appreciate) its order, only he knows which plants need how much water and sunlight, which can grow together peacefully and which require their own space to properly mature. None of us could care for it or recreate it. It truly is a miniature jungle he has amassed with determination and pleasure. Even now, at 9 AM he is outside watering them with a lukewarm cup of Dunkin' in hand. Shirtless, as usual.

My mother's fingerprints are in the interior, which screams of her personality, everything looks expensive but most of it was bought on the cheap, it's neat on the surface but messy if you really look into the corners. A quick fix that satisfies the average eye but not the more discerning. Her style is a combination of artfully arranged and over-stuffed artifacts. There are far too many photos of us and a few little old prints that make me sad, like this one, the only photo she has of her dad. I pick up the tiny 4 x 3 black and white photo no doubt taken in Cuba framing someone who clearly gave her and I our faces.

Why must I look like the family we know nothing about? My features are an amalgamation of both my parents with my mother's as clearly dominant. I put down that photo and inspect a different one, one of her as a child. This one is in Spain, I can tell. I see a little neglected girl with curly hair and a short dress, probably her only one at the time, who was so bored she used to make up fanciful stories. My grandmother often recounted this one where she ran away and was almost kidnapped by gypsies.

Despite growing up in Miami, a city that constantly celebrates its Hispanic heritage proudly, my own Spanish and Cuban roots are like background decor to me. They are places that exist on my parent's shelves.

And then there are the little black and white prints of my dad as a child. He looked like a happy, weird kid in his photos. These are all taken in the U.S. evoking the cheesiness that defined America in the 50's. There's one of him, my personal favorite, posing in a Native American headdress, moccasins and a brown tunic holding a tomahawk, so clearly a relic of a different America.

Fresh smile lines soften his eyes and denote a different childhood than my mom's, a happy one with two parents around. However, both of his parents died in his twenties, orphaning him far too young even if he was technically an adult. Actually, he was the same age I am now by the time they were gone. I don't know what I'd do in the same position.

My dad's family was from Cuba, and before that Spain we assume. Not much more is known. My Father keeps his past to himself to a laughable degree. I don't think it's on purpose, but every few years he reveals something that is shocking to us. Once he let out a casual comment about having lived in Virginia for some time. A revelation shared only because we were reading something random about Virginia. *Who even are you?* is a question my sister and I ask him often.

So, somehow, we grew up Spanish because that was all we had to work with. But it always seemed like it was all part of my imagination. Like feeling Spanish was as much an act of creativity as fact, if only because of the information I had to go off of.

When DNA kits became popular, I remember debating purchasing one for my father as a Christmas present. In part, because a few months back I wondered where my grandfather, my dad's father, was originally from. He was only alive until I was six, and I had been looking at his photos, much like I am now. Where is this man from? I honestly wondered as my eyes squinted looking at his photo. He had very dark brown skin, curly hair and was extremely short for a man. His physical traits didn't seem to place him in any obvious ethnicity. So, I asked my dad.

"Spain," he said, sounding sure. But I've learned to question when my dad sounds too quickly sure of something.

"But where?"

"Ehh, probably the North." This was highly unlikely considering his skin tone, so I had to press.

"Okay, but how do you know?"

"Well I'm assuming, most people from Cuba at that time were Spanish and that's what I heard when I was young."

"Dad," I couldn't help but feel a bit frustrated he never asked more about this. "What did your grandparents look like?"

"I only ever knew my mom's dad, you've seen photos of him."

"What about photos of your father's parents?"

"None."

"So," I said. "You're telling me that your paternal grandfather could have been from India and you would have no way of confirming or denying that? Like, you truly know nothing about the country of origin for your father?"

He took a breath.

"Well, Cristina, I guess I'd have to say no I really can't," He paused again considering what I assumed were the weight of those words. How don't we know our history?

"Listen, could you help me with my email? I locked myself out of my damn Apple again... and you know, this technology is really Mickey Mouse. Steve Jobs would be rolling in his grave."

We never did the DNA test. My sister and I decided it best to save that for another time in the future. No need to add more drama to Christmas. Maybe when we have kids? We'll see. Somehow, I've come to accept and enjoy our heritage as a slow series of revelations, like a movie we honestly don't know the ending to. I imagine it to be an M. Night Shyamalan film with a surprise twist no one saw coming, not even my dad.

"Cristina, it's time," my mom interrupts my thoughts and hands me a garbage bag.

I dutifully put my coffee down and nod, "I know."

***

Three hours, four throwaway and keep piles later, I stumble upon something wonderful. It's an old costume I wore as a kid for Hispanic Heritage Week.

"Wow," I put it down, texting a photo of it to my sister.

Do you remember?

LOL. I will never forget.

In grade school, my mother had to make a costume every year for the Hispanic Heritage Week parade they organized at my school. Although most kids were of Hispanic descent, every small child enrolled in our private Catholic school walked that parade in front of the entire assembly line representing a Hispanic country.

Having morning assembly was part of my life for 11 years. For five days a week, my entire school, Pre-K through Eighth grade, would line up standing in rows facing the small stage-like gazebo the principal and several kids would address us from. Mostly it was announcements about upcoming events and saintly days, it was easy enough to tune out, and then we ended with a prayer in unison. I always felt a bit awkward and also, we were in Miami, so it was almost 100 degrees most of the year. It seemed cruel to make us all stand frying in the sun sweating in our already unflattering uniforms during our pre-pubescent years. It was worse during these special events, like the Hispanic Heritage Week parade, that would prolong everyone's presence there.

Nevertheless, once a year every year, the younger kids would dress in the native attire of an assigned Hispanic country and parade themselves in front of the entire school— right after the prayer, of course. The parents would get to hand make a costume because Party City doesn't carry traditional attire that is highly specific to a Hispanic country or region.

The year I was in second grade, we actually got to choose our country. I really wanted Mexico. I came home with a photo of a Mexican dancer in an elaborate ruffled dress with bright pinks, yellows and blues. I was actually excited about this. I knew in my bones this would be the best costume there. Maybe even one of the best costumes I'd ever seen in my life. I came home and presented my photo proudly but also earnestly. Even as an eight-year-old I was considerate. I knew it was a tall order, but it would be so perfect if only my mom, with the help of my grandmother, could recreate its elaborate, splendid beauty.

My mom and grandmother stared at the photo of the Mexican dancer like I brought a bag of human shit into our home. They did not share my enthusiasm for it in the least.

"We're not Mexican," my grandmother finally said after a long pause looking at the beautiful Mexican woman like a cockroach. "We're from Spain."

This was a distinction I had not made in my own naive innocence. "Aren't Hispanics all kind of the same?"

My grandmother took a long sniff as if to calm herself down

to ward off her forthcoming stroke and so she could answer me in a way that wasn't cruel, "No. No we are not all the same."

My mother jumped right in with suggestions and compromises like the true Libra she is, "Well, maybe you could dress like a Sevillana dancer," she said with vivid excitement as she opened the encyclopedia for S things and showed me a photo.

Okay, now this I can work with! Sevilla is a city in Southern Spain, the region of Andalusia, known for their beautiful unique Sevillana dances incorporating castanets. Although she wore only red, no other bright colors, the Sevillana dancer's dress was ruffled too and it came close to capturing the spirit of my inner Mexican.

My grandmother again sniffed deeply looking now at my mother and I both like we were dragging shit all over our living room floor. "We are not from Sevilla; we are from Oviedo. That's in the North."

Again, a distinction both my mother and I seemed to gloss over. My mom didn't say it, but I could tell she was thinking it: Aren't Spaniards all kind of the same?

It's only now, after visiting the country, that I understand my grandmother's disdain. Spain is made up of 17 autonomous regions. Although Spain itself is a country, believe me, according to each and every citizen of its 17 regions, this is only a technicality. We are Asturian before we're Spanish. So, to my grandmother, a proud Northerner first, Spanish Citizen second, overall Hispanic person third (and dead last), the notion that her grandchild would dress like a Sevillana was just as ridiculous— if not more — than dressing like a Mexican.

Sofi was six at the time and sat idly by watching and playing with the photo of the Mexican dancer until my grandmother snatched it from her. It was as if to make sure its secondhand stink didn't intrigue her. "You both will be Asturian farmers. Lourdes, drive me to *Calle Ocho* so we can buy material. I know what to do."

The finished product was a black hat, which resembled a flattened sombrero, a white blouse that hung loosely with a big red skirt, red socks and small black shoes. I looked like an early settler; it was an observation I knew better to keep to myself at this point. Did I enjoy the parade? I did not. I waved at the crowd as dozens of elementary school kids wondered what Hispanic country dressed like the Amish.

That's probably when my heritage faded into somewhere unused and indifferent in my mind. Most people in Miami know where they are from and proudly recount stories of it. For me, it was only six years ago, when I was nineteen, that I visited Spain for the first time and got to experience at least one part of my roots. It was well beyond the threshold of creating an identity around it, but it was a start.

"Oh, this costume," my mom said, coming in and picking it up. "I forgot we had it in here."

"I can't believe you saved it," I said.

"I save everything important," she said, gently folding the garment. It'll go back in a box of childhood stuff we probably won't open again for years. These are the best moments to resurface the things of our past. Although it slows the process down, that's one thing I love about moving. I never rob myself of the moment to stop and recount an object's story with vivid detail.

"I'm ready," I say, closing the last of my boxes.

***

Bunched in the rental van, I can barely see out the sides of it. Do I really own this much?

"Dad, hand me your phone. I'll punch in the address," I say, stretching out my arm.

"Here you go," my mom hands me his iPhone. I already know I'm doing this more for me, I'll get to remind my dad every time he is tempted to deviate from the route that this thing calculates for traffic.

"Here, Mom," I hand it back. She props it up on their phone stand. Although my dad rented this car only this morning and for one trip, he already has a tangle of chargers and earbuds and the cell phone stand he brought in from his car. Since I was young, my dad's cars have always looked like the back of a TV set: a mixture of indiscriminate wires that seem totally unnecessary until the day someone needs one of those chargers and he will not let you forget it.

Gire a la izquierda, the map announces loudly in a robotic Spanish I have never heard.

"Why is she in Spanish?" I ask my dad.

"Why is she asking me to make a left on US1?" he asks, ignoring me. My mom is ignoring both of us and playing Candy Crush on Facebook.

"Dad, remember, the thing takes traffic into account," I remind him.

"But that's gonna put an extra 5 miles on our ride," he waves his hands at me.

"Maybe, but there's probably traffic the other way. Just listen to her, please."

"Fine," he makes his left turn a bit resigned.

Twenty minutes later, just as Google maps predicted, we arrive at two twin towers facing each other right off Brickell Ave, the heart of Miami's Downtown. To its left is a jungle of buildings, public transit, people in suits going to work. To the right is the entrance to Key Biscayne, a beach just a short 10-minute walk away. There's an attendant that must let us in.

"This is it?" my dad said looking back at me shocked.

"Yeah!" I am so excited I cannot hide it. "That's Lou, just tell him apartment 3A. He'll know."

My dad drives up to the little house and Lou waves. "Good morning! May I help you?"

"Apartment 3A," he says flatly.

"Oh, come right in! We've been expecting you. If you pull up right to the front, the doorman will help you with your bags and here's your assigned spot," he says handing us a sheet of paper.

"Thank you," my dad says, still looking confused.

"What's wrong?" I ask figuring he'd be happy knowing just how safe I'll be.

"Nothing, it's just… different than I expected."

We pull up and two men in uniform open our doors. "Hi there," they say in unison as they help us out and direct us to the luggage carts, which are the fancy ones they have at nice hotels.

We pack up most of our things, "Don't worry," said one of the bellmen. "You can leave the car here and come back down for the rest."

The lobby looks like something out of the architecture magazines on my parent's coffee table. There are tropical trees in intricate pots, large windows, tall ceilings, a piano in the corner and various leather chairs. It is a bit dated, like most of the older buildings on Brickell Ave, but that is part of what I like about it. It has the Art Deco look from Miami in the first wave of its glory days.

The elevator opens up to two hallways with a tasteful green carpet lining the floor. We find the direction for 3A and my dad seems more calm. Perhaps, this building isn't as nice as it seems.

I stick the key in and a large living room with sliding glass doors facing the pool and ocean reveals itself. The sunlight is reflecting off the marble floors.

"You've got to be shitting me," my dad mumbles. It's a statement for no one. He walks around the room, looks out the window and sighs loudly. "Okay, then. Let's unpack."

My mom comes in behind me. She's forgotten she's mad and where my dad sees the point in our story where I never move back home, my mom sees potential.

"We can do so much here!" she squeals. "I hate the couch but it's free, so that's good. Yes, we can work with this."

A few hours later, I am settled in. I offer my parents a glass of wine but that is too much too soon for my dad. As the day unfolded, it became clear he was counting on me living in squalor then getting tired of that and moving back home to his tropical oasis out West. One thing is accepting that fact, it's quite another to share in a glass of wine celebrating it.

"No, your mother and I really need to be getting back home. I gotta water the plants and feed the cats," he gathers his keys and several chargers.

"Well, okay then," my mother says half-heartedly. She would have taken the wine. She never says no to an invitation.

"Bye sweety," she kisses my cheek. "Text us when your roommate gets in okay?"

And just like that I'm alone. My roommate won't be here until tomorrow. We don't know each other too well but she used to live with Cassandra in college. It's a perfect arrangement. We're close enough to know we won't be weird and yet far enough removed to keep boundaries. I pour myself a glass of wine and step out on my balcony.

The wind rustles my hair. It's 6 PM and the sun has started to set but there's still light out. At this time of year, we have another hour of daytime. I can hear a few children playing in the pool and see a few adults tanning and reading, and, is that? I think that's a hot tub. Oh, yes, I can get used to this. My first adult apartment. Did I splurge on my budget? A little bit, yes.

We were looking for apartments that would mean each of us pitched in $800, but for only $200 more each this gem became available. It was an act of destiny how this apartment, my first adult apartment, came to be mine. Normally, it would not be in my budget, but my roommate's grandmother lives in the building and mentioned a vacant apartment. We figured, why not look?

That was the day we met our landlord, a wealthy Puerto Rican housewife, who didn't want to get rid of her furniture or bother selling her apartment. She wanted an easy solution before she left on a trip on her yacht. She was a stocky woman, as many Caribbean women are, but pretty. She had perfect highlights and nice scarves. She was more interested in our story as two young single girls trying to make it in Miami than getting her money's worth for the ocean-view apartment.

"How Sex and the City," she said in her Puerto Rican accent. "It's yours! What's your budget?"

"$2,000," I said without thinking.

She considered it. "$2,100. My husband will want to know I negotiated."

And that was that. I drink in the Cabernet and my accomplishment. Maybe it was luck, but I did it. I'm here, on my own.

7
Deadlines and boy glow

We are late on four deadlines, but our creative patriarch has no care. I have a hangover so bad my head is pounding. I pop in two Advils and do my best to focus. Part of me worshipped this type of mindset before, it seemed like a push back to the man. However, this is, ironically, what it's like working for the man, only our man is an extremely disorganized self-loathing artist.

"We're gathered here to discuss a very special campaign. One that I think we can aspire to ourselves."

Here we go again. Everyone is intuitively aware this is a time waster. One by one they each silently cringe as he begins to play the same Apple commercial from the 90's. He'd rather dissect this relic instead of working on the very real deadlines we have for our clients.

Everyone is nodding. Normally, I'd be annoyed. But today, I find it amusing, which has less to do with a revival in work interest and more to do with last night. I went on a date and it was good. I begin to doodle a small armadillo on my notepad. This meeting, like most, is going nowhere, but my armadillo sketch skills are improving considerably.

"Yeah, I think it's really great."

"Good stuff."

Three hours later the meeting concludes without any real direction. We've all said vague sentences about branding, which is the most malleable word I have ever heard. It is truly the shapeshifter of marketing. You can pretty much use it as filler.

"I'm gonna pop out for a sec," I tell my co-worker.

Sometimes I walk outside and look at the traffic during my break. I see people freely moving around and it makes me feel tethered to this office. I don't know where they're going, but I want to go with them.

My phone vibrates.

Had a great time last night 😊

Me too 😊

I don't know if we'll last forever or even go anywhere for that matter but having a solid first date puts enough clouds in my head for my imagination to run wild. The man in question is a Thor-like specimen to behold. He has all the right genetics and features.

As I type in today's status sheet, I imagine how good we look in photos together. His blonde hair and mine, both our light eyes, we are straight up couple porn. Or we could be, if that's where this goes. I have to hope it does, otherwise it kills the daydream.

"Hey, you look great today," my coworker passes by and says.

"Thanks love," I say smiling.

It's the boy glow. Everything looks a little better when you're in lust. It's been a long time since I've been in love. For a while it's all I wanted. I yearned for who my olive-skinned lover could be. These days, I'll settle for the similar euphoria of a good old-fashioned infatuation. I'm tempted to ask myself what the point is, but I don't want to ruin my good mood.

I go back inside over to our small printing room and pick up a copy of Ad Age. I love that they order the physical magazine, so I always read it. I have a small collection at my desk because I know the days when this will be available are numbered.

I always dreamed of working for a magazine in New York City. I loved reading and the idea of many people collaborating to put a physical booklet together. I wanted to be a part of it. But I wasn't born of the generation that would get to do that. If you work in print now, you're only useful to a dying industry. It'll all be replaced by web sites and apps. Still for today, I like to go to my desk and read this physical magazine imagining that I am living in a time that writing well matters because people read, storyboards are done with your hands and seeing that large billboard towering over the sky is the epitome of making it in the ad world.

Another text comes in. It's Cassandra.

Hi friend, drinks later tonight?

Sounds great 😊

It's amazing how happiness expounds energy levels. I've barely slept. I had a raging hangover up until an hour ago, but I am on cloud nine so going home alone to my apartment seems like a waste of a good mood.

We pick a new bar known for its craft beers. Regardless of this, I order our usual for now, two Jack and Ginger Ales. I typically hate the moments you have to wait for someone to meet you out. I feel the glares on me as I wonder if people think I'm here alone. Perhaps, she has no friends but still wanted to treat herself? No, of course not. It's perfectly logical to wait for a friend to meet you out. It happens all the time. Just in case though, let me pull out my phone and look like I'm reading.

Hmm, Mercury retrograde. Fucking fantastic.

Watch out for slick Casanova's. Be careful with your heart under this planetary backstroke. Your sign is a sensitive one opting for tradition instead of modern-day sexting and casual dating. We're not saying don't have fun but put it into perspective. As Mercury rules the past, an ex can come out of the woodwork. Remember, this is a time for pausing and reflecting not starting something new.

What a buzzkill. Of course, I know what I'm doing. Thor and

I probably won't amount to much. I'd be silly to believe that. It's all fun and games to imagine our photos splashed over social media, but I know deep down he's not the one. I can be casual though. I mean, why not? Where has sensitivity and tradition gotten me to? I'm in my mid-twenties. Sure, he's not my future husband, but when the fuck am I going to meet that guy? I take a long sip of my drink.

"Excuse me, I'll take another."

"Hey, my friend, sorry I'm late," Cassandra says kissing me on the cheek and setting her stuff down.

"Don't worry, friend. How are you? Did you know Mercury was retrograde?"

She rolls her eyes as she slithers into the barstool next to mine. "You don't have to remind me."

"How was the hospital?"

She breathes heavily. "It was intense today. I have a patient who is this lovely little boy. He's so bright, Cris. Really smart. But his home life," she pauses to take a breath and purses her lips together in a disapproving way. "I don't know. It's days like this I need to learn to disconnect."

"I'm sorry. That sounds horrible, but you're doing good work. He's going to remember you."

"I really hope so. How was your day?"

I giggle. "It was another soul crushing day in front of a desk, same as yesterday. But I started to work on something."

"Yeah?"

"It's nothing really, but it's starting to grow."

"Okay, growth is good." She squeezes a lemon into her cocktail.

"Well, it's this book. I think. I don't know if it's long enough. Maybe it will be. Anyway, it's something I've slowly been working on in between my down time at work, which is a ton. I really feel like I'm channeling something. It kinda started off as just something to do. I don't even know where it came from. I didn't have a plan. And now, it's developed into a story, my own made up universe."

"That's amazing! Really. I mean, you're writing a book!"

"Ah, I don't know. That sounds too official. I mean I'm still recovering from the blow of not making it into one of the 10 fucking MFA programs I applied to."

She waves her hands. "That's the past. Besides, you knew it wasn't meant for you. It was already written."

I shrug. "Yeah. Guess you're right."

"She knows all things. I'm telling you," Cassandra laughs.

"Well I hope she was right about my love life. It was all over that table and I still can't figure out who my olive-skinned friend is. I've made this mental lineup in my head of men who are my friends, 'not my type' and tan with really short hair. Literally, zero."

"Maybe you don't know him yet?"

"It's a possibility, but I'm starting to realize you can't really be friends with men. I mean, you can, but they always end up wanting something more from you, you know?"

She nods. "I completely understand. Have faith though. How was your date last night?"

I perk up. "Great. He's so good looking. I don't think there's anything else there but he sure is fun to look at."

"Fun is good," she laughs and sips her drink.

"Yeah," I say. "I have a sneaking suspicion I want more and will eventually get bored. I'm kinda tempted to quit while I'm ahead and not waste my time, but I'm really trying to be the person who lets herself enjoy it."

"Yes! It's an experience. Have it! Enjoy his hunkiness without having to categorize him or expect more of him. Sometimes a hot guy is just a hot guy."

Cassandra is good at this in her own way. She says she's able to separate sex and love, but there is a part of me that doesn't believe anyone can fully do that. Even with the most casual of romantic endeavors some feelings are bruised or hurt when one or both parties don't want the same thing. I don't think anyone gets out unscathed. That emotional bruise terrifies me. It holds me back from experiencing some men physically or otherwise. I've had enough scarring to last this decade. Two heartbreaks were enough to mend without going for an almost certain third.

My mom told me something wise once: Never settle. If you are not 100% into the person you choose to be with, you're not outsmarting anybody. Eventually, even though you think being the person who is less into it will emotionally protect you, once it ends you will hurt just the same as if you were fully in love. It could be the ego, it could be because people grow on you, but whatever the case, don't ever commit unless you're all in. I believe this. I've been with other men for less time and it hurt me just the same. That's why I haven't been in a relationship in years.

"How about you? How's the kid?"

She laughs. "He's good. He's there. I just saw him last night."

The kid is someone my friend is seeing. He looks like a child and sneaks into her bedroom late at night.

"Yeah?"

"Yeah," she says, smiling mischievously. "I can't explain it. We have this connection. The sex is great. He gave me this book and it's really changing my life. He's a lot more intellectual than I expected."

"Really? Wow."

"Yeah."

"You better be careful. You might catch some feelings by accident," I say, playfully poking her in the arm.

She takes a sip and laughs, "I know."

The principle is already at work. Cassandra will never give him what he wants, but she's grown affection for him that won't make the Band-Aid easier to rip off. This weird emotional bond-but-not is a wasteland. I know because I've been there. Tethering on the tightrope of are-we-or-aren't-we is the worst. You think it's fun and casual, especially if you're the one who doesn't want anything serious, until one day you find out what was temporary is not so temporary and now you need to break it.

8
The call

I finish my first glass of wine and look at the time. It's 7:30 PM.
I have an hour and a half until this call. It's windier than usual on
my balcony and I keep fidgeting from my nerves. I hate when
people say we need to talk instead of just calling. Who does that?
Just call.

I had a one-night stand. I knew what it was, but he didn't.
We're twenty-five, so I thought it was about time to go on with
it. The olive-skinned friend is nowhere to be found, so why not
play with the other options my card reader so thoughtfully
provided me? So, I did. I knowingly slept with Brian, the second
man the psychic told me about, and now we need to talk.

When I make a bad decision, I like to take the opportunity to
really let myself have it.

The mistake itself may have only taken a moment, maybe a
night as did the decision I am currently mulling over, but its
remnants will likely haunt my mind for months or years.

It was a bad idea, and now, instead of preparing myself for
the phone call to address Brian's feelings about the fact that we
had sex, I'm pulling out my big ex box, a crate containing all

material evidence of my first love. Obviously, I enjoy deep pain and discomfort. There's no better way to prepare myself for a serious adult conversation then to go back and revisit the first fuck up of all time. My first, AJ.

But before all that, I need another glass of wine. I get up and refill my glass from an open bottle, presumably my roommate's. Hopefully, she won't mind, but fuck it, she used my hookah yesterday without asking.

"Why do I even still have this?" I say out loud to no one in particular as I open the box my mother encouraged me to keep, insisting she would save it for me— only when I moved out she decided to convert my room to my Dad's office so she kindly brought both my ex boxes and hid them in my apartment, right above my winter coats (all the things I need never unpack in Miami). The message was clear when I moved: You want your own apartment? You want to be a grown up? Take your baggage with you, emotionally and otherwise.

I pull out a photo from the small box. There he is, blue eyes, long dark hair next to a much younger, blonder version of me. These days, I'm rocking more of a natural honey blonde versus the platinum California Beach blonde of my high school years. It felt a fitting choice for early adulthood, like somehow the darkening of its shade would allude to wisdom accrued. I don't even recognize this other girl in the photo. She's long gone, but I do remember this green T-shirt. He wore it the night we first met.

House parties were all the rage, and this was one for the books. My high school friends will agree, top five for sure. The night began like they all did, at my friend Cheryl's house, a girl I haven't seen since that time in my life. We both went to a private high school that was considered more off-the-grid. I liked that about it, plus we were co-ed, unlike a lot of the private Catholic high schools. But what I enjoyed the most was that I didn't have a reputation at these parties. I could be anyone. None of them would know, would they?

At my school I spoke to practically no one and had my head buried in my phone texting all the people who were my friends at the other schools. In my weekend world, I felt a semblance of what it was like to be connected, something I never was at any school I attended. This disparity was strange. I used to attribute my outside popularity to being able to be myself, something that was difficult to accomplish at my own school for whatever reason. For all of high school, two days a week I would go out and be the person I really wanted to be. Maybe even the person I really was.

It's not that I was a nerd. I blame my real-school disconnection on the fact that I treated being there like a job. I clocked in and clocked out. I never raised my hand. I seldom made conversation with people in the halls or between classes. I was always looking forward to everything that happened outside of there. My real life had nothing to do with where I went to school despite spending technically most of my time there.

The night I met AJ, I sat cross-legged at Cheryl's house getting ready. I was putting on thick black eyeliner to accentuate my green eyes, a trend at the time, as Cheryl decided where we'd go, or rather, her friend Janey who went to the main all-girl school did. She heard of a big house party in Cocoplum, a ritzy neighborhood close to the ocean, so off we went. In Miami, there are the moderately wealthy, these are the people whose kids went to school with me. And then there is another level, a separate batch of elite private schools, the ones whose tuition runs in an entirely different tax bracket. The owner of this mansion was part of the latter.

"Wow look at that house!" I said in genuine disbelief as we pulled up to the coral mansion standing four floors above us with landscaping I'd only ever seen in hotels.

"It's fine," Cheryl said. She never let herself admit anything was better than her or out of her reach. Her and I both lived far away from the wealthy neighborhood our school was in. Our parents lived in comfortable homes out West. We were middle class, another point of bonding for us since most of the kids at our school were rich. She'd never acknowledge it out loud though.

She was beautiful to me. She looked older on account of her height and slender figure, something I desperately wished I had. At 5'1, I was petite and had the body of a young boy. Most girls in Miami were my height, which helped, but the height and baby face combination always made me look younger— which kept me in the cute zone. It shocked me earlier that same night when upon finishing my eyeliner, Cheryl turned to me and said, "Wait. You can't look better than me. Give me another 10 minutes."

Something about the exchange felt off, but my fragile-cute little ego barely paid notice to the glaring sign that it was. Instead I felt flattered. I was a chump.

We walked into the party and the crowd was a mix. There were faces I recognized from the main private schools, even a scattered few from my own school, but mostly it was kids from the elites. Their outfits were impeccable, all the girls looked like they came out of a magazine with perfect long hair— not a single frizz in sight despite Miami's moisture-rich air— and loose beachy tops made of expensive fabrics. I suddenly felt like my budget Brazilian jeans and tight Forever 21 black tank top was sophomoric at best. Cheryl felt the same, I could tell.

"Let's get a drink," she took my hand with all the confidence of one of them. I probably looked like a deer in headlights.

At the keg, I saw him. His bright blue eyes shining in the faint lights from the house. He couldn't stop staring at me and it made me nervous. I actually felt my chest turn red and was immediately grateful it was dark.

"Hi," he said.

"Hey," I smiled.

"Oh, you haven't met AJ? AJ this is Cris," Cheryl said casually pouring herself a beer and scanning the crowd.

"Would you like a refill?" he asked motioning to my empty solo cup.

"Sure, thanks," I said. "I just started drinking the stuff. Still getting used to it."

He laughed. "It takes getting used to. It's a Yuengling keg though, so this shouldn't be horrible. At least it's not Natty Ice."

I had no idea what any of those words meant yet. "Yeah, for sure."

"Where do you go to school? I've never seen you around."

"Nope. I go to school with Cheryl. I guess we're from the random school," I said half giggling.

Coldplay's Yellow began to play. It was a slower pace than the punk rock and reggae playing before it, the signature sound of that time. "God, I love this song," he said.

"Hmm. I'm not sure if I've heard it."

"What?" his eyes widened. Shit, that was lame. "Let me get your number. I'll burn you the album. You need to know it."

"Here you go," I said as I handed him my phone. "And thank you kindly for saving my musical taste. You're a gentleman and a scholar."

His eyes shot up from my phone as he let out a surprised smile. "You know I don't speak Spanish, Baxter." He threw me another line from Anchorman and we both laughed. "I like you." he said.

And then his big blue eyes were lit up once more, but this time by the blinking blue and red lights of a police car. The party was about to be raided.

Cheryl came up to us, "Hey guys, guess we gotta go."

AJ looked at her and then me. "Well, we may head to someone's house. Call us?"

We got into her car after passing the cops who looked more annoyed than seriously concerned. Breaking up house parties in wealthy neighborhoods because of noise complaints was probably boring for them.

We never went. Cheryl wanted food, and by the time he called back, everyone we knew at the party had gone home.

"Aw, all right. Guess we'll call it," she said before hanging up the phone.

"Was that AJ?" I asked.

"Yeah," Cheryl said. "I saw you two talking!"

"Yeah," I said shyly.

AJ texted me a little later. I was sleeping over Cheryl's house and remember vividly smiling under her thin sheets as I stared at his message from the soft glow of my Nokia.

It was really good to meet you. Good night.

It was AJ's style to ignore the rules and be romantic. The love letters I have in this time capsule are proof of that. When we broke up, I wanted to burn them in a ritual of letting go, except my mom insisted I keep it all.

"This is all you'll have one day," my mom said picking everything up and packing it into a neat little box. "You'll want to remember this time in your life. I'll keep it for you. You won't even need to see it."

And yet here I am on the precipice of a very uncomfortable phone call regarding my sexual transgressions opening up a big ol' box of AJ.

I am a physically younger version of my mother. She has a dainty voice and a Spanish accent. Her hair is brown, my natural color, and her eyes are a similar green shade. Her skin is much more olive than mine. It's a natural tan I wish I would have inherited. I've been trying to replicate it since I was thirteen by lathering myself with baby oil and then frying in Miami's unforgiving sun. It's only now that I realize the years of damage I've inflicted upon my poor skin, the results of which I likely won't see for years to come.

My mom had only one other boyfriend her whole life besides my dad, and she was fourteen. Did it even count? I always thought when she'd tell us stories about him. I never interrupted because I could tell for her that really is what she had to remember her past by. A small piece of it that was only hers, since she married my father at seventeen years old. A part of me always thought I would follow in her footsteps. Perhaps not the whole getting married as a teenager thing, but certainly the high school sweethearts turned lifelong partners part. Having spent most of my high school experience in a relationship, it was a natural assumption I'd be one of the girls who were "lucky enough" to tie the knot early in their twenties. Of course, that wasn't the case. I would go on to break up with AJ and date around in an effort to find myself just like the rest of us, keeping many of my early adult years all to myself.

And now I'm here checking my phone awaiting this dreadful call nowhere nearer to finding "the one." I'm not even sure I will anymore. It's 8 PM. I still have time. Brian said he'd call me at 9 PM. Maybe I'll put something funny on TV so it's not that depressing that I'm opening my ex box and drinking wine alone. Amy Schumer comes on.

I know this bit. This is the one where she looks in the mirror and wonders, *Am I gorgeous? Am I only a haircut away from being really gorgeous?* I laughed so hard the first time I heard it because I've been quietly asking myself that my entire life. It's the embarrassing truth. I've caught myself staring in front of the mirror as I pout my lips and squint my eyes. Maybe this whole time I've been casually gorgeous? Just flying under the radar. If only I lose those 5 pounds.

Women aren't rewarded for having that kind of power. I was taught to be soft and dainty. I learned approachable is always better than powerful. As a matter of fact, I was once dating this older guy. He was a real bag of issues. He was the first guy I dated after AJ and he wanted to be taken care of, except I didn't know how to do that at the time. I was only nineteen. It was right after my breakup with AJ, and I needed so badly to be taken care of myself, not become an emotional caregiver.

My mom would actually help me write text messages to sound more maternal. She gave me an entire speech on how men really want mothers. She wasn't wrong. My mother knew how to capture a man in that way. But I was born different. The caregiver role would be a learned behavior for me. I always felt like an outlier until I paid attention to my dad. There's nothing comfortable about him when feelings are involved. It's this weird 1950's thing about him where feelings aren't expressed out loud, they are tolerated in solitude and preferably with a smile.

I'm more like my father in that sense. Crap, what time is it? 8:30 PM. I still have time. But maybe I should put all this shit away. One by one, I put letters and photos back in the box and then I find one from when we got back together. This was from college. God, that really was devastating.

There were signs I ignored because I wanted our second chance to be it. I spent all the years between our breakup trying to get over him, but all roads always lead back to AJ. My heart never could let go of him. Even now I don't want to admit that. The biggest sign happened on a day we went back home. At the time, we were living in Gainesville, both of us were away for college. That weekend we were back in Miami and went to a birthday party at a friend's house. Everyone from high school was there. I think that's what made him snap.

Our love had been rekindled in Gainesville, a place so different from Miami and separate from the people who saw our story from beginning to end. It was a safe space to let our guard down. Back at home was another thing entirely. Being around the old friends who were there when we dated the first time was a strange feeling. Maybe they weren't thinking about it or maybe they were, but we were aware that everyone there saw us break up. They saw all the bitterness that ensued. They saw who I was with after. They saw who he was with after. They saw us go to the same places without acknowledging each other's presence. It really did get ugly for a time. And that night, they saw us walk in holding hands and being a couple again. It was tough to ignore the feeling that maybe everyone was talking about us, or at the very least didn't know how to approach us.

He didn't want to be at the party, and he did nothing to hide it. I was shocked at how bitter he was acting in public with no care that other people around him could tell. A strangely familiar knot formed in my stomach. It was a reintroduction to something else I didn't like from our past. When he decided the party was over, it was over. There was no amount of cheering him up that would save the night.

I was desperate to please him. It's a pathetic feeling that comes from being given a second chance and wanting to protect it like a butterfly in my hands. All the while everyone looking at me knows the one thing that is obvious: once you touch the wings of a butterfly, it's dead. The thing was over before it began.

We got in the car and I could feel the tension.

"What's wrong?"

He didn't even look at me. I saw his fists clench on the wheel. He'd been drinking a little bit.

"Hey, what's wrong?"

"Tell me again who you were with while we were broken up." His eyes didn't leave the road.

"What? Why does it matter? Who cares?"

"It matters."

"I'm not mad at you for any of the girls you were with!" My voice rose. I didn't want to give in. I knew where this was going.

"Answer me!"

There it was. That scary yell. I'd only ever heard it a few times.

"I was only with one person." I could feel myself pathetically giving in. I just wanted it to stop.

"What's his name?"

"Why does it matter?" my voice quivered while tears filled up my eyes.

"Who was it!?"

I tried to be quiet for a while hoping he wouldn't ask any more. It bothered him so much that I was with someone else. I knew it was the timing. It was too soon after us.

"Answer me," he became calm again.

"Ray."

"Him?" He screamed even louder. "How could you?" His voice went so high it was hoarse.

He knew the answer all along. He had me hand him the permission slip to do what he had wanted to do all night or maybe ever since we got back to Miami, the environment he nursed his broken heart in.

"You knew this. Why does it matter now? You slept with people too!" I said, dry heaving, but he showed no mercy. I think he may have been a little bit happy to see me squirm.

We drove back to Gainesville that Monday and it was over.

I haven't taken many emotional risks since, except for Adan, of course, who nursed my heart after my second breakup with AJ. It scarred me for so long, that final ending, all its dysfunction and ugliness and shame hung around me for years. It isn't until now, on the evening of my first conversation involving casual sex, that I note how utterly unfair and misogynistic it was for him to be downright furious because I slept with someone else. Meanwhile, he saw no wrongdoing for being with other women, including my friend Cheryl, which I came to find out later. The psychic was right; I wore the stench of that anger and resentment like a thick coat.

I've done it all backwards, spending my formative years in two long-term relationships, forcing me to now learn what it is to be single in early adulthood. Like most of my peers, I don't have an arsenal of experience to fall back on. I had exactly two men who were committed to me in high school and a great love that came quickly and intensely at the end of college. So, now I get to struggle my way through the nuances of lust and to what extent it's okay to explore my sexuality while remaining a lady.

This is one of the principal differences of my twenties compared to a dude my same age. Whether or not anything but my old Catholic guilt tells me so, my lecherous aching is like a dog on a leash that only goes so far. The concept of what I'm doing always hits me in the moment and gives me a nun-like reflex. At best, I have been called an uncrackable code among friends and suitors, at worst a tease.

Which brings me to exactly where I am now. Waiting for a phone call and having zero experience in the implications of a one-night stand. Tell you the truth, my sexual escapades have been limited and complicated, always mired in feelings and promises. I want to be able to give in and let sex be what it can be, but years of being raised to associate sex with love have indelibly marked my psyche. My vagina and my values are always at odds, and both are quite stubborn.

So here I am, third glass in at this point. It's 8:55 PM and my anxiety is through the roof. I've managed to distract myself with every piece of convoluted history I could possibly remember and I'm no closer to knowing what I'm going to tell Brian. I turn off the TV and begin pacing around my neatly closed ex box. My only ever one-night stand and I choose a friend? Damn it, Cris. Couldn't you have chosen a random? He wouldn't have cared this much.

Of course, you didn't, I see myself in the mirror. You coward. You wanted that emotional buffer, you wanted to eliminate the risk of rejection. I know he's liked me for years. I recognize the pattern because it's the same pattern all my closest male friends fall into. I used to act like this was a happy accident.

Celeste calls it my, "Oops I did it again" syndrome. I've heard her warn a few guys before we become close to be careful. *She's a man-eater*, she'd say. *She'll never go out with you*, she'd warn. *Take a ticket and wait forever.* And still, every significant, close male friend in my life has ignored her and approached our burgeoning friendship with a doomed sense of confidence only men have.

It's only now that I know I've created this. I never realized my confusing craving for intimacy and sex would play out in my male friendships. I flirt, sometimes intentionally, to fill the void I'm too afraid to have in relationships. And then, I can't show the same seductive skill with any of the men I actually want to be with. I'm incapable of committing to it. It's not as safe as the friend zone, my favorite place to explore closeness ever since I was hurt long, long ago.

I never had sex with any of them though. Despite our togetherness—which in some cases extended to regularly making out and sleeping in bed together holding one another—no carnal knowledge was shared. Until I fucked that up last Saturday.

Brian's text hit me unexpectedly while I was at work last week.

Hey, would you go to dinner with me tonight?

I was sure I should say no, and yet I told him yes. I thought I could handle it. I was a little sad that things didn't work out with Thor, so I figured, what the hell? I've been on so many close encounters with friends before, even vacations where we stayed up till dawn talking about philosophy, monogamy and then slowly tracing the shape of each other's lips with our tongues. None have resulted in sex, how bad could dinner at a Vietnamese place be?

But dinner led to wine back at my place, and Brian went for it. So, I did too.

On the old couch that came with my furnished apartment, he held eye contact with me a little longer than normal and then kissed me for the first time. The kissing was good, which surprised me. He picked me up and carried me to my bedroom, which really surprised me. Then we did it. It was awkward and charming in the way I'd expect it to be between friends who'd never seen each other naked, but also good.

There, I thought in the moment, my first one-night stand. It took me halfway into my twenties, but I finally managed to sleep with someone I have no intention of being with.

"You'll probably forget about this and go back to normal, huh?" he said in an obviously hopeful way waiting to be corrected.

"Probably," I answered.

Then he got dressed, hugged me and left. I didn't feel used or bad, I felt fine. I didn't expect to feel that way. I didn't expect to be able to separate sex and feelings.

A week went by and I didn't reach out to him. Then I received a long text message earlier today that took me aback. He told me I treated him like some guy I met at a bar. He told me a lot of things I didn't expect. For years, I've gotten away with casually disconnecting until the other person caught on and followed suit. I have tactically avoided any meaningful encounter that forced me to kill the one thing seduction's staying power thrived off of: hope. I know I could not deny him, my friend, a real conversation after we opened up Pandora's box.

The phone finally rings. It's 9 PM.

"Hey," he says. I can hear the road's soft noise in the background. He just got out of work and he's driving.

"Hey," I say. My hands are literally trembling. I can't distract myself anymore. "How was work?"

"Pretty good, you know, the usual." He pauses. "We're small talking pretty hard, eh?" he laughs.

He's funny. Could I like him? It's a shame I don't. I love his ability to diffuse a situation no matter how tense. It's part of his charm. I imagine him smiling with his whole face. It's a sweet face set on a milky white foundation with baby blue eyes and light brown hair. He's handsome in an approachable way.

"We sure are," I say laughing. "Talk to me."

"Well, you know I've liked you. This isn't new. But I felt like you threw me away the way you pretended it wasn't a big deal we got together. It is a big deal, you know?"

"I know," I said softly. "I'm sorry. I don't know how to do this. I've never done that with anyone outside of a relationship. And I just don't think I'm ready for one so I figured I'd be casual about it, you know? Make it less awkward that we've seen each other naked."

He laughs. "So, you're not ready? For a relationship..." his voice trails.

"No, I'm sorry. I'm just not there right now." There it is. I regret it as soon as it comes out, *right now*. The qualifier that all people who lead people on say. I can't ...right now. Those two little words hold all the promise of a possibility, that maybe, just maybe someday in the future we could be together. Just not right now. But keep on keeping on.

Why did I just do that?

I hear him perk up. "Okay, I understand. Well, let's talk again some time. Don't be weird with me. Thanks for taking my call."

"Yeah, of course. I won't be. Bye." I hang up.

My heart is racing. I'd skillfully avoided answering his question: Are we, or aren't we?

This should be simple and straightforward, but it's not. This isn't just about my safety buffer; it's how much I hate disappointing people. I hate telling people no. In my naivety, I've avoided confrontations because somehow it feels less harsh to have people arrive at their own no, rather than deliver the no myself. No feels so heavy, so final. I have a hard time committing to anything final. What if I change my mind and this no spoils it? What if we can't be friends and he dislikes me because of the no?

I think I'm off the hook until I hear my phone vibrate and a text glistens through the screen in the night's light.

Do you think you'll ever like me that way?

My shoulders hunch as I type the words I know will hurt but I have to say.

No. I'm so sorry.

I step out onto my balcony wine still in hand as I take a last sip looking out to the ocean that always calms me. It looks like a big black blanket marked by shiny white sparkles when the waves move and the tall streetlights reflect off it. Seems as good a place as any to question the kind of person I am. Maybe a coward, maybe cruel. Maybe in my own goddamn right to have sex and choose for that to mean what I want it mean. Maybe someone learning to finally fess up and say no when it's warranted.

Growth is a complicated thing. I've always categorized myself as someone who is mature beyond my years. I've been told that time and time again, reinforcing the idea. However, I'm not sure if that's true. The more I age and experience, the less I find myself well-versed in. The more I learn, the less I seem to have known. I tell myself I'm brave, but I feel like a coward. I tell myself I want to be in love, yet I keep creating the exact wrong conditions to make that happen.

Do I need all the answers right now? I thought I did. Maybe it's okay to be in the questions.

9
Game Changer

Saturday mornings are quiet, especially this early. My roommate and the girls she went out with are dead asleep snoring off their sins from last night. I am always up early anyway, sinner or not.

I impatiently stare at the coffee drip, it's a small cheap coffee maker I've had since college. It does the trick but it looks misplaced against the marble countertop and floors and stainless steel appliances.

I get my cup and peer out to the living room. Two girls and a dude I don't recognize are strewn across the couches and floor. Okay, coffee in my room it is. I go back and shut the wooden door, careful not to wake anyone. I open the bright windows and settle in my bed. It's a small bed close to the ground. We pushed it by my window, so I'd have a perfect view of the pool and ocean. It's like waking up to a vacation every day.

I've been getting home earlier and earlier these nights. My roommate and her friends stay out till morning time. I catch myself yawning at midnight maybe 1 AM. It makes me giggle. I used to have screaming matches with my dad to let me stay out later. I fought tooth and nail for half an hour or even 15-minute increments to my curfew. Now, I'm basically following his curfew when I have all the freedom I want. That's life. I wish they would have let me enjoy it more when I had the desire to do it. No harm I guess, nothing good happens after 2 AM anyway.

I love mornings. They're filled with the most hope for me. I don't care about being alone. In fact, I prefer it. Once the day progresses and everyone is out with plans and friends and partners, that's when I get uncomfortable. It all of a sudden becomes more depressing to be alone.

I have to change out of my PJ pants and suddenly I'm aware of my body again. I look in the mirror squeezing my baby fat and sucking in my stomach at various angles until finally letting it out. It is what it is, I shrug, and then try to pick out something that makes me feel pretty. If I'm lucky, I'll have something I want to do, but these days that's rare. My friends will invite me on boat days but that's basically my nightmare. They never fully know the owner of the boat and that guy is usually a jackass. I went once and I vowed never to go again unless I know everyone. I had been sitting at the bow of a boat when we saw a huge 4-foot wave ahead. We figured the driver would slow down, but again, I didn't know him.

We were just girls going on a boat and so it didn't matter to him who we were, nor to us who he was. We were accessories, expendable. He ramped the engine full steam ahead and the boat violently hit the wave. I could actually hear the noise of the boat smacking water. It was terrifying. We flipped three feet above our chairs, nearly falling off the side. I turned back to face the driver and I must have looked so angry. He didn't care much. I was a boat girl. The rest of the day my friends laughed and continued being grateful for the sun and the opportunity to be there. I sat and realized what the fuck I was, a boat girl. I barely drank or enjoyed the day until I got off. That was the last time I was ever anyone's accessory.

My friends are still in that stage. Their early morning hours after coffee are spent texting and calling, trying to get on a boat. They invite me all the time and I refuse. I'd rather find something else to do or literally stay here by myself. I guess I don't much like the daytime unless it's the morning. Once happy hour rolls around I begin to feel good in my skin. I am slimmer in evening attire and I like going out early to the bars in downtown. It's these daytime hours in between that don't suit me.

***

I can hardly believe it's 6 PM when I hear my friends yell my name. Cassandra comes into my room and lays over my bed, her body tanned from a day out in the sun.

"How was it?" I ask sleepily. I'm waking up from a nap.

"Great, it was a beautiful day. You should have come," she says while texting someone.

"I was able to lay out by the pool a bit, and then I came back up and did some writing."

"Oh, nice! Well, you gotta come out tonight," she said. "I'm not taking no for an answer."

I could already feel my laziness objecting. "Well, I dunno."

"Cristina Alejandra," she says my first and middle name with emphasis. "You are not staying in tonight in those moomoo pants. I refuse to let you. It's my duty, as your friend."

I look down and back at her. "Fine." My moomoo pants are a pair of PJs no man should ever see me in. They're two sizes too big with flying cartoon cows. "I'll go shower to wake myself up."

"That's the spirit!" she slaps my butt.

Two hours and two pre-drinks later, we are approaching our usual spot.

The city's lights shine in the darkness of an early sunset. Bars and lounges are fleeting in Miami with expiration dates so quick, sometimes I wonder why people bother opening them up. A pink neon sign with a black bird drawn into the name hangs over the bouncer.

"ID please," the large man says as he holds our licenses up to his face. He has the same nondescript identity of most bouncers, right down to the black shirt and pants.

He does a body scan of the group and hands us our IDs back. It's more important that we look a certain way than if we were born a certain date. This is Miami. In other places like Europe, bars let you right in. Unless you're in a big city, like Madrid, you don't need to look a certain way or fill a certain female-to-male ratio. No ID checks over there because drinking is so widely accepted regardless of age. Here, we cannot wait for a taste. Tell an American that they can't have something and it becomes the object they desire most.

Everyone is sipping cocktails and beers, taking shots and humming about the bar. I always get an adrenaline rush walking into a bar. Part of it is the anticipation of what could possibly happen. I could meet someone new and be whoever I want. It's not just being hit on and the promise of Mr. Right, it's the reinvention of myself. It's the first day at school as the new girl. Most people find that uncomfortable, but I revel in it. Once you know people for long enough, they label you with their problems. They project onto you what you make them feel and despite knowing that's the case, it bothers me anyway. I'd rather be in control of who I am and how I am perceived to be. Or at least I used to be.

Right now, that same rush is coursing through my body, but I feel the other side of the emotion: anxiety. I wish I could feel that excitement for what this night could be and even more who I could be in it, but I don't feel driven by the same desire to wield perception. I don't even care what people assume. I'm nervous.

"Drink, my friend?" Cassandra moves us to the bar.

"Yes." I don't know if I want one but it's a habit.

"Two vodka tonics! Extra lime, please!" She screams at the bar tender.

So, it's that kind of night. I was hoping for the slowness of a whiskey drunk, but I don't correct her. Maybe I need something to take this edginess off.

"Thanks," I take my drink and begin to stealthily crush the lime until little fruit particles swirl around the ice.

"So, how are you?" We make ourselves comfortable, staying close enough to our friends but just out of earshot.

"Honestly, I'm feeling weird."

"How so?" she tilts her head and listens while keeping an eye on the bar. She's multitasking. She's doing what I would be doing only I don't want to because I'm nervous.

"I don't know. I feel a little strange. Even right now. Usually, I want to go out but I'm feeling uneasy."

"Really? Do you wanna leave?"

"No, no. It's fine. I'm just not feeling up to, you know, doing the thing."

She nods, settling back into her position, her eyes scanning like a submarine. No target yet.

"Oh, goodness," she says, and that's when I see him.

Adan is here. The sight of him and the smell of smoke at Blackbird takes me back in time. I can smell the cigarettes and beer of the Spanish bars we used to frequent together. I could smell the whiff of fried food mixed with sweets from fresh pastries in the bakeries lining the streets, the strong aroma of an espresso. All the things we smelled when it was time to leave and grab a midnight snack. It makes me ache for him in a way I forgot I could.

A renewed shiver runs through my body at the prospect and familiarity of him. It would be so easy to fall into a night of nostalgia, to go right up to the one man who I know finds me desirable. To do all the subtle things I know will drive him mad and feed my hunger.

My body moves towards his long, lanky silhouette and abruptly pops to a halt.

Let it go. The words are ghostly, but I hear them. The psychic told me Adan is good. He was wonderful to me and he healed me after the catastrophe that was AJ. But this is my past. I see her light blue eyes looking directly at me reminding me of this. He is not your future.

"I'll be right back," I say to Cassandra. I move towards him trying to get the psychic out of my mind. It's not like I can't say hello. How rude would that be? Now is the perfect moment. He's standing between friends but in a position easy enough for me to talk to him one-on-one.

"Hi," I say.

"Hey," he says, hugging me so closely I can smell his cologne. Another familiar spicy scent that brings me back to happier times. "How are you?"

"I'm good. Just grabbing a drink with Cass." I smile, beginning to tuck my hair behind my ear and then remember I hate how that makes my ear look, so I start pulling some strands out to casually cover it.

"I saw," he says, nodding in Cassandra's direction. "How are things?"

"Good, you know, the same. How's your family?"

He tersely smiles. "Better. Good."

"That's good." I let out a bit of a laugh. It's the laugh of someone who knows your story, who knows exactly what "better, good" really means.

"I'm gonna go say hi to these guys and grab a drink. See ya around?"

"Oh yeah. Go for it. See ya around." I turn, looking for something to do. The conversation was shorter than I would have wanted. Usually Adan is up for the nostalgia, especially in this context. It's probably for the better. I knew going up to him should only be what it was, a simple exchange of courtesy among people who used to know each other.

He walks away and I feel somewhat relieved. I don't know that I would have had the self-control to leave him in the past like I know I should. Going back to revisit old history, even good history, is never the way to move forward. It doesn't make sense and it hasn't helped me. I'm always trying to find love, the future, by re-visiting my old wounds, the past. I'm never in the one place where everything possible resides. Right here. Right Now.

Speaking of right here right now, where the fuck is Cassandra? I lost her to some guy she found on the other side of the bar, so I decide to order another drink for myself, though I have little desire for it.

The bar is dark. I can barely make out the people standing by it. A neon glow touches their facial features just enough to reveal their attractiveness or lack thereof. God, what a rat race. All these people are scanning each other. This is my spot though; in the past few years, I've picked up quite a few guys here just like this.

I become embarrassed suddenly recalling a memory of the last time I was looking for the bartender and trying not to meet eyes with a particular man on the other side of the bar.

I'd just gone on a bad date at a high-end restaurant on Miami Beach with a guy I met right here at Blackbird. It was called The Meat Market, a fitting title for a first date.

My outfit was wrong because I didn't know where we were going. His outfit was wrong because of his misguided sense of style, and the server gave us a condescending tone most of the evening. I began to see all the imperfections my friends pointed out to me when I had given him my number. I sort of knew, but I was an optimist. If someone made me laugh or had any semblance of a redeeming quality, I always figured under the right circumstances there may be something there.

But all I could see was how big his nose was despite having a handsome face. I saw him stocky, not built. I noticed he tucked in his shirt, which was a Polo and that reminded me of my dad. He was respectful and genuine, which made me feel all the more guilty that I figured out at dinner I didn't like him. He dropped me off after we ate and my friends were at my place getting ready to go to Blackbird.

"Uh-oh. You're back way too early," they said in unison

looking up from the mirror where they were putting on makeup.

"No-go, guys," I dropped my purse onto the dining room table.

"Oh well. You're dressed. May as well come out." I figured, fuck it, why not?

I was standing more or less where I am right now when I noticed him across from me. We had both decided to get back on the horse and keep searching. Our similar determination makes me think fondly of him. Perhaps we had more in common than I thought. We awkwardly avoided each other the rest of the evening. I probably should have just stayed home. I probably should go home right now.

"What'll it be?" The bartender interrupts my daydream with his curtness. My pause already annoys him.

"Nothing. Thanks."

I spot Cassandra. She's still working on her guy. I tap her lightly.

"Heyyyy," she smiles widely as she drags the word. She's tipsy. "This is Derek."

"Hey there," Derek extends his hand. He looks like he's in a boy band with gelled black hair and dimples dotting his smile. Not normally her style. He doesn't seem annoyed that I've interrupted. Maybe he's actually nice.

"Nice to meet you. Hey, I'm gonna get out of here, I think. You good?" I ask the two universal words for *do you need saving?*

"I'm good." She doesn't.

"Okay, text me when you're home." The code for: still not sure if this guy is a murderer, so confirm you've not been chopped into pieces and dumped into the Miami River, please.

"Will do." Message received.

It's wintertime in Miami so I'm not sweating outside. On the contrary, I'm a bit cold in my tank top as I stand next to the bouncer. He looks considerably bored under the pink light. It's late now, people are drunk. He doesn't need to hold the line outside so young people passing by assume this bar is where they should be. At 2 AM, everyone's good and drunk. They need no convincing to walk in. Except for me.

He nods his head. I return the gesture. A few groups of scattered beautiful drunk people walk by. I feel insecure for a moment standing by myself. Some people walking by look at me.

I set up an Uber and I'm tempted to stay on my phone. Surely, she's texting a friend and waiting for them on this corner, they'll think. Seems reasonable. But I stop right before, forcing myself to remain phoneless and present as I look out at the street.

My Uber finally pulls up, "27th and Brickell, please." I forgot to put the exact destination in, perhaps a sign that I was being present? I'll take it. I feel myself jolt back as the car thrusts forward. Everything flies by quickly in a mixture of bright lights, tall buildings and the faint sounds of people wandering the streets in search of their next conquest.

How much longer can I really do this? I'm wasting money and time trying to fill a longing that seems impossible. They make being single seem fun on TV shows but I'm 0 for 10. I'm exhausted from the mental gymnastics, *is he or isn't he?*, the wardrobe changes and nights out playing a part. When does it start to get fun?

***

The next morning a text comes in. It's Cassandra.
Good morning my friend. Happy July.
Morning 😊 How was the rest of last night?
It was fun. How are you?
I'm here. Trying to begin the day with positivity and failing. You?
Same 😊
Yoga?
Let's do it.

Does it count to drink wine in workout clothes and think about yoga? This is what we're doing now.

"But we're working out the mind," I point to my head.

Cassandra lifts her wine glass. "We most certainly are."

"I'm having a hard time deciding what I want," I say.

"Go on," she says.

"Well, I just feel so stuck. I'm focusing all this energy when I want to find my 'purpose' all while there's this bigger void inside me that isn't filled either. I want to be in love. I miss feeling loved by someone. And this stupid want is drowning out my ability to think clearly. It keeps me in this frustrating state of inaction."

She nods taking in my story. She is studying psychology after all. I can see her excelling. She's a good listener. "I think the answer is you have to love yourself first. Accept yourself as you are right now and give yourself that love you crave. The purpose will follow soon after."

"Ugh I don't want my love. I can barely stand to hear my own thoughts," I said, drinking a bigger sip of my wine.

"That's the fucking problem right there!" Cassandra says, taking a bigger sip of her wine.

We both crack up. She's right.

"Do you love yourself?" I ask.

She considers it. "I do but it's hard some days. I don't always give myself love. I struggle with being quote-unquote selfish. I struggle with owning my power. I struggle with acceptance. I think we all do."

She's so good at stating her problems without telling the specifics. It's a skill I hope to master one day. I don't feel jipped, quite the opposite, it makes me feel like I blabber on too much giving away mundane details of my life while not getting to the point. Am I that old grandmother who goes on and on about the details of her hip surgery while someone politely nods until she's done? All the while they really only needed to hear that she is recovering both physically and mentally and she just wants to be in someone's company?

"I don't think you're selfish. I think you're discerning with your time," I said, standing up pacing with my wine. I know where this one comes from. It's a narrative her family tells her. I have the same one from mine. "I mean, if someone wants your time and you say no, a healthy boundary, and then they get mad, doesn't that make them selfish?"

She considers it. "Yes, actually."

We both nod and stare off in silence. It's a full moon tonight. If you believe in it, and I do, there is potent energy during full moons. Energy, as Einstein said, can neither be created nor destroyed. It must be converted. Full moons can be a scary mesh of everyone's energy that tests you or they can be rife with opportunities you can alchemize.

"Look at the moon," I said, staring up at the sky.

She nods. "It's scary."

"Yup," I say, sipping more wine. I know what she means. We've both been in it lately. It seems like circumstances beyond our control are blowing up everywhere and we can't seem to alchemize any of it.

"I'm done. No more trying so hard. No more pushing. I surrender," I say, looking up again at the stars. "You hear that, universe? I surrender. Do what you will, I relent. I can't keep fighting."

"I'll join you," Cassandra replies. "I surrender!"

"To fucking July," I say, clinking our cups to what is hopefully a new month with a fresh new start.

"To fucking July," she says.

10

The Golden Opportunity you are seeking is within you

The feelings of hopelessness and heartbreak have taken me down all sorts of unorthodox paths. I can understand how patients suffering from chronic diseases seek treatment outside the realm of logic, rubbing smelly ointments on their bodies or doing any other number of nonsensical things even though they have only a vague promise that this will heal them.

Having given up the game in the name of July and all its promise, the next logical step is to work on purging myself once and for all of these nagging heartbreak thoughts... through black magic.

"I have something you can do," Cassandra tells me. "But only do it if you believe it. It's going to sound a little weird."

"Try me."

Cassandra lights candles for me and instructs me to go first. We are going to perform a personal ceremony of cleansing our auras. The ritual has roots in Santeria, or Way of the Saints, an Afro-Caribbean religion many of the locals practice. Santeria is a mixture of Yoruba, a religion from West Africa, and Christianity, specifically its Roman Catholic form. This blended faith was born in Cuba during the slave trade, and since most of Miami is Cuban, it made its way here.

You can find chicken bones and flowers next to altars with statues of saints right on someone's front yard. That sort of thing is normal. I've been to many office buildings and seen a glass of water strategically hidden in the corner of a room, an offering to the saints to watch over them and ward off those who mean harm. Santeria is everywhere in Miami. It's not just those who wear the all-white signature uniform and openly share their altars who practice it. Apparently today, I do too.

I fill up a small bucket with water, white petals and a splash of perfume. It's taking all of my nerve to remain serious, am I really doing this?

"Go in the shower, bathe like usual, but at the end you're going to dump this bucket over your body. Sit with it. Feel your intention. I'll be on the other side," Cassandra smiles and closes my bathroom door.

There is no harm in such a minor representation of what I have longed for, I think to myself, so stop feeling weird about this. Succumb to the ritual and the freedom that comes with it.

The shower is warm and I'm wondering if I'm messing this up by thinking about it. Should I not think about it? Let me go back to my intention. Dear God, hmm, well maybe that's not exactly a good place to start. If the God I learned about in school knew what I was doing I'd be on his shit list.

I can hear my parents now, "All those years of private Catholic school and now you want to be Jewish?" They said to me incredulously in college when I informed them I was not Catholic and I would be shopping around to see which religion was right for me, if any. This was deeply offensive to them, even though they weren't practicing Catholics. They were really more Easter Sunday Catholics than anything else.

"You can't shop for a religion like you do shoes!" my dad huffed. In the end, it turned out none of them were right for me.

Dear spirits...shit.

"I'm in the shower, Cass! Can you please use cold water to wash your hands!"

Where was I? I'm lonely. I'm stuck. I want to be loved. I want to love myself. Isn't that the reason we're all here? To love and be loved? Please, if you could find it in your heart to let this ridiculous offering work, I swear I'll be so good. I want to be free.

I turn off the water and dump the bucket's cold contents all over me. It's fucking freezing. Immediately, small goosebumps feel like they're cutting through my leg and what is supposed to feel spiritually and energetically liberating is more like a prison shower.

The smell of my cotton candy perfume wafts in the air as I open the glass door to step out and quickly wrap my warm towel around myself. In my bathroom candlelight I see Cassandra brought all my lucky elephants and stones. Between the makeshift altar and the white petals in my shower, this bathroom looks as crazy as I feel.

"Holy shit. I'm really losing my mind."

"How's it going in there?" Cassandra calls through the door.

"Feeling clean– literally and figuratively!"

She comes in.

"The symbolic purification was a washing over of the past and looking forward to a bright future," Cassandra says shimmying around my body holding a bucket of her own in one hand and lit sage in the other. "See you in ten."

***

Oddly enough, we celebrate this ritual by going back to Blackbird. I dunno what it is about this place and why we always end up there, but I don't have any resistance in me left. I am surrendering. So when my sister opts to join us it makes the decision easier. Screw it. The day can't get any weirder.

We make our way in and the line is shorter than usual. Even

the bouncer seems to be in a better mood.

"Hi girls," he says, revealing a big toothy smile.

We smile back as we each dip into our purses to fetch our IDs. He interrupts us: "I've seen you around. Don't worry, come on in." He even opens the door.

"Thanks," I say, shoving all the makeup I never use, but pack just in case, back into the thimble with straps that is my purse.

"What just happened?" I yell over the music into Cassandra's ear.

"Magic," she says, pointing to the back patio. We shimmy around all the sweaty bodies.

The brightly-lit patio is an area I usually avoid. It's easier to hide away inside Blackbird's cloak of darkness and the safety of sitting on a stool and blending into the bar. As we claim our small parcel of land to stand on with minimal pushing and shoving, I see a familiar face in the crowd.

"Oh man! It's Jacob. I haven't seen him in forever!" I say, squinting my eyes.

"Really?" Sofi says, looking around delighted. "My God I haven't seen him since the night we got tanked at that hookah bar in Madrid."

"Heyyy," Jacob says as he hugs me. He always gave really good hugs, they're the type of hugs that linger just a little longer than normal. The sign of a person who's comfortable with affection.

"Jacob!" Sofi gives him a hug. "It's so good to see you. I'm gonna grab a drink though, see you in a few?"

He looks mostly the same. His brown hair is visibly thinner and shorter than it was years ago, but his skin is still tanned. His big brown eyes have the same feeling of kindness. He smiles revealing one dimple on his left cheek. I never noticed he only had the one. It's an attractive quirk made more pronounced by his muscular jawline. He has a few more lines around the edges of his eyes and mouth than I last remember. Life has marked its experience onto his smooth babyface. Damn, I wonder if I look older too?

"Cristi, what's up?" he asks, nudging my arm. The name takes me back. For the last few years I've been Cris, a more grown up version of my name whose gender ambiguity has been helpful in the work world. Everyone from the high school era of my life knew me by that juvenile nickname though, a nickname I quickly changed at my job when I wanted to be different.

"Not much, working at the same place. I moved around here though, so that's been cool." I say, motioning to the street.

"Brickell, huh? That's fancy. You're a bonafide grownup," he says, taking a sip out of his bottled beer.

"I'm certainly playing the part well. How about you, Mr. World Traveler? I see you on my feed and get jealous in my little office. You're really out there seeing the world. You did it."

I knew Jacob had sold his things, quit his job and moved to Europe. I saw it online and there was some mention of it among friends. I was so jealous of him. I never had the guts to do something like that.

"Yeah, my trip was incredible! I can't begin to tell you all the amazing places we saw and the knowledge. Truly, it feels like I just got a Masters in life."

"Well, tell me!" I say, taking a fresh cocktail from Cassandra and mouthing the words thank you.

"I thought about you a lot, since you know, last we spoke for real was in Spain. I have so many recommendations for you. You'd have loved the entire trip, well, except the parts when we slept on the street."

"You what?!"

"Oh yeah, towards the end there we were running out of money and it was rough. This one night we had to sleep in a garage, and I thought we'd get mugged."

"Jacob, no way, really? Oh my God. You're nuts!"

He laughs. "Yeah, it was fine though. Really, I wouldn't trade the experience for the world."

"Geez, I thought I had it rough when Cass and I stayed in a

hostel with shared beds. Kudos to you, my friend."

"Did you ever read that book?" He asks, taking a sip of his beer.

"I did," I say, putting my hand on my chest. "Thank you. It actually really helped me. How crazy that it all took place in Miami, huh?"

"Right?" he says, taking another sip. "I mean, right over there if you think about it."

"So what are you doing back here? I thought I saw you were in North Carolina for some time. Did I make that up?" I ask, recalling seeing some photos of his life post-Europe in the mountains.

"Yeah, so I moved back in with my grandparents for a few months. They live in Bryson City, it's this really small town in the middle of The Smokies. Just trying to clear my head, make my next move and spend time with them while I can."

"That's so sweet. You know, I used to have lunch at my grandma's every day. Her place was right by my job. It was really special. You gotta enjoy them."

"Oh totally," he says. "I'm so glad I did. They're getting older. I actually love where they live. I went hiking every day, I went and studied for my GMAT at the local coffee shop. It's the perfect little town, only not for a young single person, you know?"

"I bet. Though I dunno how great Miami is a place for a young single person either," I say, half laughing. "It's rough out here. I'm thinking about moving somewhere else honestly."

"Really?" he said, raising an eyebrow.

"Yeah, I haven't even mentioned it to anyone actually, but this month I had this moment of clarity and I sort of gave up— in a good way. I surrendered, is a better way to put it, and I'm starting to think maybe this city just isn't for me anymore."

"Wow," he says, looking intrigued. "Where will you go?"

"Oh God, no clue! You're the first person I've told. The idea just popped into my head today really. I love Miami and I come here all the time," I say, motioning to Blackbird. "But I think I've outgrown the best it has to offer me."

"Man, I know exactly what you mean," he says, nodding and looking off. "I'm actually finding I appreciate it; I could use a bit of the hustle to get back into working."

"Well, my friend, you will find plenty of that," I say, clinking my glass to his bottle. "There is no shortage of the rat race here. We are a sea of nine to fives, bars and single people. From one soldier in the battle to another, I wish you luck."

He laughs. "Fuck, in some ways I feel so ahead and in others I feel so behind compared to everyone, you know? My friends have been building their careers and meeting their wives, and that's awesome, but I've been going on a personal soul mission. So, on the one hand, I feel like my awareness is through the roof, and on the other, I feel kinda like I'm starting from scratch."

"Well, it's all relative," I say, considering his position. I feel the same in a different way. "Is one area of development really better than the other? In the end, we'll probably all end up just fine. Don't get me wrong, I can't follow that advice for the life of me. But I think it's true, deep down."

"Guys!" Sofi interrupts us. "This place is getting super crowded, why don't we go back to Cristi's place?"

My eyebrow twitches a little. That damn name.

"That's cool with me if you're good?" Jacob asks.

"Yeah, why not? Actually, I do have a bottle of absinthe I saved from our last trip to Europe."

"No way! It's a sign. We have to drink it," Jacob says, putting his arm around me. "I'll tell Aaron. He's gotten lost somewhere around here but I'm sure he'll be down. Text me the address?"

"Perfect, see you in ten."

We pack into Cassandra's car and make our way on the road. It's a short drive to my place from here. Five minutes, tops.

I text Jacob: Confetti to 420 brickell avenue

Confetti?

Typo.

Everything's better with confetti though. Especially absinthe.

Touché.

I giggle.

"Uh oh, what's that?" Cassandra asks.

"Nah, nothing. It's Jacob. He's just funny is all."

We pull up to my building and park. On the way up, Cassandra smiles at me. Sofi is texting behind us. I hear the sounds of our heels clacking against the shiny tiled floors.

The boys find us at the elevator. "Any trouble finding the place?" I ask.

"Nope, perfect directions," Jacob says, raising an eyebrow. "Confetti helped."

Cassandra shoots me a glance and I ignore it.

"Who's ready to get weird with some absinthe?" Sofi says. She's always good for the hype.

"I am!" Cassandra raises her hand as she opens my door with her key. At this point my apartment is a sorority housing several of our friends on rotation.

"All right you guys take a seat outside if you want while I get us some glasses," I say, making my way to the kitchen. It feels grownup to lead people into my own apartment that I pay for and say things like, *Oh I'll get the glasses.* Never mind that they're all mismatched shot glasses from college.

The balcony is usually a place I longingly stare at the ocean in question of life's big decisions. Just a few hours ago I was there drying off after my voodoo shower and reaffirming to myself that I am not, in fact, losing my shit. These are the actions of an open, experimental adult. It's windier now that it's nighttime and we are in the midst of a pivotal conversation: what do we do when the inevitable zombie apocalypse arrives in Miami?

"We arm ourselves, obviously," Aaron chimes in. He is somewhat of a zombie expert, on account of his obsession with comic books.

"You know, maybe we should build those blocks people have

in their doorways!?" I suggest.

"What blocks?" Sofi asks.

"Dude!" I say, raising my cup and getting ready to lay down some second-hand knowledge. "I'm still not totally confident this is true, but I heard some people 'door block' their apartments as a way to zombie-proof it. They basically build a block you have to step over to get inside. They do that because, get this, zombies can't bend their knees."

"That's actually true," Aaron adds, trying to explain to us the legitimacy of this architectural oddity, but we're too busy laughing so hard our faces are frozen in a hideously silent scream.

"This isn't a joke," Sofi says, moving her jaw around to get the feeling back in her face. "I'm convinced the man who ate the homeless guy's face was not on bath salts. That was a zombie attack if I've ever seen one."

She's talking about a big news story, the latest to make Florida our nation's strangest state. A homeless man was attacked by a tourist who literally ate his face. The homeless man was hospitalized, the drugged man was killed and we were all meant to believe bath salts are to blame.

"You know," I say, taking another baby sip of absinthe. "Maybe he escaped from some government lab where they were experimenting with zombies. We have no way to tell— the cops killed him on the scene!"

"No amount of drugs will ever make you eat a living person's face," Jacob says, nodding his head as he rolls a cigarette. "That was definitely a zombie and we need to be prepared." He lights it as he makes one last point. "I think we need to get them in the heart or head, right?"

"Yes, exactly," Aaron says. "It's the only way to kill them."

"I'll take a shot to that," Cassandra says.

We pour another round.

"To surviving the zombies!" Sofi yells, making me somewhat concerned that the other people in my building probably don't appreciate our balcony party, but what the hell, this apartment is to be enjoyed.

Three AM rolls around quicker than we expect, so we say our goodbyes to the guys. Cassandra, Sofi and I crawl into my queen-sized bed. Finally, we take off our bras, remove our makeup and put up our hair. It feels really good after such a long day.

"It was nice seeing everyone again. Can you hand me the Advil?" I say rubbing tea tree oil on what seems to be an incoming zit.

My sister tosses me the box after taking two. My body does not handle hangovers gracefully, or at all, actually. There's a part of me that longs for the yesteryears of irresponsibly binge drinking without the following day's punishment. We're only given a finite number of hangovers our body naturally circumvents in our lifetime. Mine ran out in college.

"It was nice seeing Jacob again," Sofi says. "You could use a friend that isn't in love with you."

***

Monday morning always comes too soon. The marble floors are cold underneath my feet. It always makes me do a few little hops as I go make coffee in the kitchen.

Every day I have the exact same routine before work. Make coffee, wash my face, brush my teeth and sit on my old man chair watching the sun come up over the ocean.

I don't know when we began to call it the old man chair, it's a lazy boy with a dated swirly pattern in burgundy and dark brown. I used to find its pattern so offensive, I'd cover the whole thing with a blanket, which looked ridiculous. I've since come around to accepting the things I cannot change, like this chair and the rest of the furnishings that came with the apartment. That was part of the deal after all, our landlord wanted it easy. She did not want to deal with moving out her old man chair, her dated beige couches or the huge TV entertainment center that looks like something out of the 80's.

A text comes in. It's early for that. Usually most people are in their morning routines.

Morning! It was awesome catching up with you.

It's Jacob. Interesting, what's he doing up?

Hey! You're up early? Same 😊

Getting into the grind 😊 You busy this weekend?

Not really. What's up?

I have extra tickets to an art show. Wanna check it out? They have free drinks.

Yeah, why not.

Cool. Send you the info later. It's Friday at 6 PM.

And just like that something to look forward to. Spending time with Jacob is a good move, a sign to the universe that I'm finished with the chase. Normally, if a friend asked me to make plans on a weekend that was anything outside of going to a bar, a place to meet people, I'd reschedule it. I never wanted to waste a prime social night filled with potential. But now, I think I'll choose to spend time with friends and figure out my next move, maybe even literally. If I do go somewhere, I'll miss the days of simply spending time with them. I'm done chasing, I'm ready to focus on me, to flow.

BEEP BEEP BEEP. Time to go. My mornings always seem to end too soon during the week.

The drive to work is quick. I'm at the office early, fresh coffee in hand. It's dark in here. I like it.

I power on my laptop and check my horoscope.

This week there is a full moon in Aries.

I'm listening.

Aries is a fire sign. For you it's time to awaken the passion and fire inside you. What could you do to ignite excitement in your life? You may just discover it during this lunar cycle.

Well that is an interesting proposition. What could I do to make things more exciting? For starters, disrupt my routine way of thinking. Case in point, taking off a typical Friday from the rat race of single life and instead go see art with a friend. I'm already feeling a shift, a certain levity I had not experienced before when all that drove me was filling a void. Had the shower ritual worked? Or is this simply what letting go feels like?

My phone vibrates. It's Cassandra.

Hey, can you chat?

Yeah give me a sec and I'll call you.

Okay.

I grab my phone and go to my usual hiding place, the empty third floor office space in the historic building I work in. I often escape here throughout the day. Sometimes I come here when I need to be alone, to think and, on occasion, cry.

"Hey," Cassandra picks up right away.

"Hey friend, how are you?" I ask, my fingers tracing the windowsill. I look outside at the busy streets of Miami; it looks like a jungle with buildings in between the tropical plants. A living, breathing entity with roads alive like arteries, every day flowing with people getting to or coming from somewhere.

"I'm okay, in a bit of a funk. The kid is getting to me."

"Hmm," I murmur, letting her know I'm listening.

"I wasn't that interested, you know, and now he's kinda fallen off and I find myself wanting him to call. Am I crazy?" she asks, honestly wondering.

"No, of course not," I answer. "I get it. I've definitely felt that, and it sucks, sorry. And if it's any consolation, I genuinely think it's your ego that's hurting right now."

"Hmm," she murmurs to me. "How so?"

"Well, you don't like this guy. You never really did. Unless you honestly feel that's changed, and I doubt it, because I know what that looks like on you. This is coming from a part of you that wants to look good. It's the illusion of the upper hand, you know?"

"Okay, yeah, that's resonating. Keep going."

"It's not real. If you go after it, first, you're wasting your precious time and energy on a guy you really don't want, and second, I'm gonna get woo-woo, you're sending the exact wrong signal to the universe. It gives us what we put out. If you put out 'I'm chasing the wrong guy' actions, what are you going to create more of?"

"The wrong guy," she says, I can tell it's helping. I love the feeling of knowing that perfect thing someone needs to hear. She's done it so much for me; it feels good to return the favor.

"Thanks, Cris. That helps. You're right. I just feel off today and it would have been nice to feel wanted."

"I know that feeling so well," I say, laughing. "I gotta take advantage of this moment where I can rise above that and think clearly. Trying to hold onto it, you know?"

"Oh yeah. Where are you, by the way? Work?"

"Yep. I'm in my hiding place," I say, as I walk around the desolate rooms. They all have small piles of sand from the termites that are feasting on the old structure. I often open and close drawers while in a trance of my own thoughts.

"Ah, yes," she says, knowing exactly where I am. I've told her about it. In fact, just a few weeks ago I came here to cry and found a little piece of tie dye ribbon with the words *The Golden Opportunity you are seeking is within yourself.* No doubt a purposeful happenstance, but I didn't know exactly what it meant at the time. I kept the little ribbon and hung it on my desk. I think I'm starting to understand what it means.

"It feels peaceful here, like I'm pausing life."

"That sounds necessary."

"I think it is."

***

I'm downstairs.

Shoot. I thought I had more time. The week went by fast. Friday and tonight's art show crept on me.

Be down in five!

I put on the last of my makeup and do a quick scan. It's not like I have to try much, but you never know who will be there.

"Where are you off to?" Cassandra asks. I didn't notice she was here and now I see her and another one of our friends lounging on the couch.

"I'm going to an art show with Jacob. He's downstairs. I think it's in Wynwood? I'm not sure actually," I say, slipping in my second earring and tussling my hair. I'm not sure that ever really does anything to change it but it makes me feel better.

"Well that sounds fun," Cassandra says, she's smirking.

"Stop it. We're friends. I am a strong independent woman!" I say, laughing.

"You sure are," she says, laughing a bit herself. "I'll see you later Ms. Independent."

Jacob's car is a modest one, a dated Honda, much like my own. The bellman lowers his head and I can tell he's eyeing Jacob. I've been picked up by fancier cars in this very spot, but those guys are usually douchebags. The walk down always feels nervous right at this point, the seconds between the building door to the car. I'm never sure where the night will go, if I'll feel comfortable or how much conversation will flow. I'm appreciative today that I don't really need to think about that.

"Hey there," I say, opening the door.

"Wow, you look great," he says, coming in for the customary Miami cheek kiss.

"Thanks! I didn't have much time between work and the show, but I figure art shows are always a bit dressy."

"Everything in Miami is always a bit dressy," he says while smirking, his dimple facing my side of the car.

"You're absolutely right. The other day I went to the grocery store in my yoga clothes and actually felt dressed down," I recount to him, our little grocery store here in Brickell is always packed and everyone is either stopping in after work or before going somewhere elegant. I live around some of the biggest corporate offices, hotels and event spaces in Miami, so everyone is always dressed to the nines.

"That's one thing I don't miss, I gotta say. In North Carolina, it was chill, you know? You can wear jeans and a t-shirt, but here, I have to find all my button downs and God forbid I wear sneakers."

"I never thought about a guy's perspective. I figured it was only the girls paying attention."

"Oh yeah. But, you know, take the good with the bad, right?" he said, making a left turn and eventually finding a spot. "We're here."

The building is one of the city's coolest revivals. In Miami, everything feels new. I love it when a structure speaks to a different era, it makes me feel like I'm there, remembering along with it. This one is an industrial warehouse from years ago resuscitated into something remarkable. Outside, the steel walls have been painted with vibrant colors, there are at least three large murals people are posing in front of. Inside is the biggest transformation, what looks to have been a place where cars were manufactured is now freshly painted with big light fixtures, mid modern century furniture strewn about and features a curious collection of artwork. It's a fantastic mixture of cartoon sketches, collages of paint splatters and graffitied canvases featuring popular slang in Miami culture. As we make our way through the exhibit following the crowd and grabbing our complimentary glass of wine, we get to an arrangement of bright canvases featuring words, like BRO, CHONGA, DAS IT, DALE, and my personal favorite, EATING SHIT.

"What am I even looking at?" I say, sipping my wine and laughing.

"Miami. You are looking at Miami," he says, sipping his wine. "In all its glory."

"This is fantastic. It's everything that makes this city an unquestionably strange mix of... I dunno actually, I'm too close to tell what it is," I say, sipping more wine and looking around at everyone else.

"Well, let's break it down, right? That's what we do at art

shows?" he says, smiling and pointing at the EATING SHIT canvas. "Only in Miami does 'eating shit' mean 'doing nothing,' and that's because it's a direct translation of 'comiendo mierda,' which is a totally acceptable way to say wasting time in Spanish."

"Oh man, that's so true! I guess that sounds pretty terrible if you don't know, huh?"

"Yep," he agrees, grabbing my empty cup, setting it down and getting us two fresh ones from a server passing by. "Your turn, explain this one."

The word GETTY is spray painted in pink on a lime green canvas.

"Okay, this one is easy. Getty is short for get-together and I haven't heard this word since eighth grade," I say, utterly delighted. "Okay what about that one."

Jacob turns around. LIGA is displayed in moody hues of pink and purple.

"That is a hair tie, thank you very much! Last one. Go," he says, pointing at a tie dye canvas with the words PATA SUCIA written in gold.

"I don't think I've ever had to explain this in English," I say, giggling. I'm feeling the wine.

"Well," he says, putting his arm around me. "What does it make you feel?"

"It makes me feel like someone is dirty as hell because this means they're walking barefoot back to their car from da club," I say, emphasizing the last words for effect. Who even am I, right now?

"Okay," he says, barely containing his laughter. "You nailed it, but I don't think 'da club' was part of that definition— technically speaking. I'm just saying."

"Oh man, are you that guy? Are you a Mosby?" I ask, pointing my finger at his chest.

"What's a Mosby?" he says, again collecting my empty cup and grabbing two new glasses of wine for us.

"Thank you," I say, grabbing my fresh cup. Thank God these are small. "It's from How I Met Your Mother, a show that'll change your life, and specifically this references the main character who is a corrector through and through!"

He takes my hand and puts it on his chest. "Oh God, I am, aren't I? That kinda breaks my heart."

I take one last sip. "It could be worse. I wouldn't sweat it."

Five rounds of free wine later and we are back at the entrance of my apartment complex.

"Good night," he says, taking a piece of hair away from my eyes. It's an intimate gesture that catches me off guard.

"G'night! Thanks for giving me your other free ticket. That was the best art show I've ever been to," I kiss his cheek and open the car door.

A new bellman is on duty and this one is less discerning. He barely sees me or Jacob, he's reading a mystery thriller. I hear the click of my heels on the floor until I reach the elevator. I pull out my phone and see a text from Jacob.

Good night 😊

Get home safe 😊

Inside my apartment Cassandra and my roommate have fallen sound asleep on the couch, an empty bottle of wine and a ton of Chinese takeout are all over our coffee table. I remove my shoes and pile them on the tiny hill of high heels accumulating at our entryway. It's a bit of a mess, but at least we are considerate not to wake each other up. I fill up a cup of water and chug it. I know better than to go straight to bed after that much wine. Tonight was fun. Maybe the most fun I've had in a long time.

I shut the door of my bedroom quietly. God, I love this bedroom. My bedroom. I should really enjoy it more. Am I thinking about this because I'm drunk? Maybe. I wipe off my makeup and look at myself in the mirror. Now this is what flow feels like, I tell myself.

The last thing I see is the streetlight reflecting off the ocean. I close my eyes and feel a bit of a dizzying sensation. Shoot, I'll probably be hung over tomorrow. It was totally worth it.

11
Confetti confession

"I have a confession. I think I like Jacob." We're seated in my apartment having some wine, and the admission spills out of me.

"What? Noooo! Cris, you're finally all 'I'm woman hear me roar.' You can't go backwards! Plus, isn't he kind of friends with AJ?" Sofi said, somewhat upset.

"I didn't plan on it. I like spending time with him. Don't you think I know how inconvenient a choice he is? I get it. Not the 'mature' 30-year-old I had in mind."

"Cris, if you're sure I say go for it," Cassandra chimes in, she refills her glass and then sits cross legged on the carpet.

"What?" Sofi says. "You really think so? I feel like she just started enjoying yourself."

"Yeah, but that's typically when you find love!" Cassandra says, waving her glass. "Happens all the time. You say you want something, and you keep asking for it and then the minute you surrender to it, the universe gives it to you like that." She snaps for effect.

Sofi's face scrunches up. Although she is only two and a half years younger than us, it's moments like this where it shows.

"I feel conflicted about it, but I'm into the guy, what can I do?" I say, sipping my wine.

"You do what you must, my friend. You go for it," Cassandra says matter-of-factly.

Jacob is by all accounts an inconvenient choice. He isn't the guy I'd envisioned in the bathroom as I spilled raging cold water and petals over my naked body willing my soulmate to find me. He is my age, in fact a few months younger, I wanted someone older. He lives at his aunt's place and doesn't have a job. I was hoping for a guy who owned his own place and had a stable job. He broke up with a long-term girlfriend a year ago, a somewhat respectable time frame but oddly feels too close considering my last serious relationship was four years ago. But worst of all, his friendship circles run dangerously close to those of my past relationships. He knows and loves Adan. He knows and respects AJ. No, Jacob is not what I had in mind, not even in the slightest. And yet, as I feel his interest in me growing into something more than friends, I find myself leaning into it.

All my life I've been a planner. I take a vision, make a list and go after that. I know from experience part of getting what you want is knowing what you want. You can't hit a target when you don't know what it looks like. My target was a 30-year-old, mature adult male, someone outside of my sphere who can get to know me and let me be me without any preconceived notions, someone who is interested in what I like. But the days following my ritual purification, a thought had dawned on me. What if we have no way of fucking visualizing who we're supposed to end up with? Or what job we want? Or anything, really? Sometimes life can surprise us with something beyond the scope of our understanding that blows our own expectations out of the water. Maybe we're not supposed to get too hung up on what it looks like because that narrow mindedness closes a world of possibilities.

So, I thought about it, I followed the string of my own reasoning. Why 30? Because I want someone mature who knows what they really want. Why outside of my current group of friends? Because I want someone to approach me with openness and curiosity, and in my experience, familiarity can kill that. One by one I broke down each "thing" I wanted in my future lover. Turns out, there are certain core elements I want, and they don't need to come dressed in any particular way.

Sure, Jacob's details don't line up with who I pictured, but his intentions are pure. In the past few weeks, we've been reconnecting as friends and he accepts me. He asks questions. I even told him about all the mystical bathroom stuff and he simply laughed. We've stayed up late quite a few nights talking about life, why we're here, all of it. He gets me on a deeper level than anyone does. Surely, it's at least worth exploring?

I heard a quote once: "If you want to be tough, be tough." What I take that to mean is the method is far less important than your decision to do something.

My life has been marked with bumpers of my own design so that I can always be safe. I never say no, I rarely take chances, I let myself explore real intimacy in a zoo-like construct of friendship so I can be in control. All of those creations were designed carefully by me, to play it safe, to look good, to protect myself. I've carefully tread on the line never fully committing myself to any person, job or identity. There's always an out, never a concrete decision. And I'm not sure how much it's making me any safer. What if making a commitment will lead to the freedom I've been desperately trying to find?

I decided to be tough.

***

We meet at a dive bar and things are different. It was supposed to be just me, Celeste and my friend Mark, but Jacob had sent me a text as I was getting ready.

I don't want the night to go by without seeing you.

It was a small but decisive step in a more-than-friendly direction. So, I invited him. I hadn't seen the harm until Celeste pointed out a glaring detail to me.

"You invited Jacob? And it's just us four?" she says, looking up from her bronzer as we make our way to Coconut Grove, a more Bohemian part of Miami that's filled with more college students and hippies than suits.

"Yeah, what's wrong with that?" I say, pulling up to the perfect spot just outside our destination.

"I dunno Cris, usually you and Mark end up making googly eyes at each other when we go out. Kinda weird if Jacob's here," she closes her bronzer and smooths out her hair one more time.

"We don't always do that. It's been awhile since we've been in that space. Mark and I are friends," I say, taking the key out of the ignition.

"Yeah," Celeste says, giggling. "So are you and Jacob."

Mark is my friend who made the psychic's shortlist of love options for me. There was him, Brian and the illusive third option, my olive-skinned man.

Mark has clung to the sidelines for years. We've been doing the *Are we or aren't we?* dance for quite awhile. It's a dynamic I have the power to turn off and on based on necessity and desire. I'm not proud of that, but I didn't intend for it to happen either. Mark has been my friend for years; we never crossed a line. I wasn't interested and he had a girlfriend for a long time. I'd always seen a darkness in him. He is cynical, yes, but more than that calculating. Mark is intelligent, but too often he uses his powers for bad more than good. He can understand how people work almost immediately. I imagine his mind as a fascinating labyrinth where he can see four steps ahead of most of us. The problem is, he'll often use this insight to his advantage, or worse, for entertainment.

"I think there's something primal about sex," Mark says, only seconds after first introductions with Jacob. It's classic Mark.

This is the only way he knows how to start a conversation, with something disruptive and triggering. He likes to drop a bomb and watch people's reaction from the sidelines. It's as maddening as it is intriguing. His intellectual discourses and complicated psyche are part of his allure, but he sure can rub people the wrong way. "It reminds me of cavemen who used to take a woman into his cave and have her right then and there."

The comment sits in the air for a little, as usual.

"Yeah, that sounds a lot like rape to me, but hey, whatever floats your boat. Cris, you want another beer?" Jacob says. It's too quick for Mark to address. What is Mark supposed to do? You can't come back from that.

Celeste whispers in my ear, "Let the pissing match begin."

As Jacob grabs my drink and Mark wonders WTF just happened, I begin to think if it was indeed stupid or callous of me to invite one line-crossing friend to the company of a prospective line-crosser. So, I decide quickly to pivot to a new environment with more people to serve as buffers. Thank God, my friend is throwing a party nearby. "Hey, my friend's having a Cinco De Mayo themed moving out party nearby. Wanna go?"

"There's nothing I'd like to do more than put on a sombrero right now," says Jacob.

"Yeah, let's go," Mark, says. He's still confused about what's going on with Jacob. I can see him doing some mental gymnastics. His eyes are always his dead giveaway. I don't think he thought Jacob was a potential suitor and now he's re-strategizing.

We walk over to my friend's house through the unlit roads of Coconut Grove. It's my favorite area of Miami. This bohemian neighborhood is filled with all kinds of thick foliage and the occasional pack of peacocks passing through. In a city being changed by tourists and out-of-towners, this place is the closest we have to the memory of Old Florida. The houses are a mixture of classic Key West bungalows and a few modern box-shaped houses, a sad sign of times changing.

"Here it is," I hear the unmistakable sounds of Mexican melodies. We walk into something that feels like a college party. I loathe Cinco de Mayo. I really do. My annoyance is not about the holiday so much as where it sits on the calendar, which is the day before my birthday. Every year, I intend to ignore this glaring fact only to find myself succumbing to a night of cheap tequila and waking up with a raging hangover.

Jacob brings me a sombrero and puts it on my head. "It looks cute!"

I smile tersely.

Mark snickers. "You sure do," he says. He knows.

Outside the tension has neutralized as my co-workers join in and we can all talk like adults who don't mention caveman sex or rape to bolster testosterone.

"Breaking Bad is a masterful achievement!" one of the TV producers at my job passionately says. We're all seated at a round table in a classic Grove patio surrounded by shrubbery, pots with overgrown plants and small tea lights above us illuminating a humid Miami night.

"I agree," says Mark. "I'm into a good guy turned villain you can root for." His eyes set intently on me. They have that uncanny ability to pierce through me communicating his message perfectly.

As I consider my response, I see Jacob's name light up my phone and I look at him. It's a text. He smiles wryly and I hide my phone under the table so the others can't see.

Let's talk alone.

How? We're at a table in the middle of a conversation...

Go use the bathroom and then come back.

"I gotta use the restroom really quick," I say without thinking about what this means.

In the bathroom, decorated thoughtfully with colorful streamers and mustaches, I find myself looking in the mirror and recalling all the other moments I come back to this very position. We seem to find ourselves in complicated times, my reflection and I. Maybe I should start looking at myself during more neutral moments, but my instinct in life's tricky situations is to find my face. A nervous, electrical current is flowing through my body. It's been quite a while since I've felt butterflies in that sweet, high school sort of way. The way you feel when someone who really likes you goes out of their way to find you alone. The past few years have been a parade of suitors more well versed in desire or the interview-style conversations dating entails to find out what we mutually want out of life. This is different. It feels like it belongs in a different era of my life, or maybe it's just been that long since I've experienced it. It's a lightness I never knew how much I missed until right now.

My hair looks as good as it'll get in the humid weather. I pinch my cheeks to add some color, gloss my lips and that's about all I have to work with in here. It'll have to do.

I come back to the table and Jacob is gone, so I look at my phone. He's written me another text.

Excuse yourself and go to the front yard.

"Be back in a second," I say.

Mark looks confused and Celeste changes the subject. "You think they'll do a sequel?"

That's the last thing I hear as I open the front gate and walk through the dirt path to the front yard illuminated by more tea lights.

"Hey," Jacob says, leaning on the front gate.

"Hey, what's up?" I ask, unable to mask my smile. We both know why I'm out here.

"I was hoping to get you alone," he says, grabbing my hands. It catches me off guard. "I like you. I like everything about you. I've thought about you since the day we met in Spain, honestly. You've been on my mind and I know we're friends, but I feel something here worth taking a chance on."

I'm taking it all in wondering back on the few brief encounters we had. It's strange to imagine he always had feelings for me then. Did he think I did too? He was the only male friend I never played those foolish games with. He was off limits to me, always. And yet, looking back, I can hear the whispers of our friends, teasing us about spending all that "platonic" time together, a farce in their eyes. Man, sometimes people really don't know, and yet here I am proving their suspicions right. Life is surprising. This is everything outside of what I strategically planned for but I feel completely at home.

I smile at Jacob. I don't say a word, but I think that's fine. It's been awhile since I've been understood so perfectly, I don't need to be the one to do the talking. It's really nice to be led sometimes.

"Close your eyes and open your hand," he says, pulling something out of his pocket and putting it in my hands. "Open them."

It's a small glistening pile of confetti.

"Everything's better with confetti," I say.

He smiles and I can see his dimple. "I'm asking you to take a chance with me and see where this goes."

And then he kisses me. His soft, thin lips navigate around mine slowly and then faster and with more passion. His hands cup my face as I continue to hold my small pile of confetti. When we finish, he laughs. "Throw it."

And I do. It falls all over the ground giving the grass and red poincianas a sparkle in the night's light.

"Okay," I say. "Let's see where this goes."

12
Revelations of reemployment

Even inside my car I can feel Miami's summer moisture making its way into my hair. Smoothing out the frizz, I recall the conversation I just had with my dad. Be careful, Cristina. This isn't the first time he's had reason to worry. I am once again driving through a shady area of town to attend an obscure interview. The psychic's prophecy had finally come true months ago, and the company I once dreaded to work for, no longer exists. In a twist of irony, I ended up loving my job. Go figure. Just as I began to really appreciate it, it went belly up. She was accurate down to the reason it folded, bad business deals.

Since that, countless odd jobs and assignments have led me here. *When are you going to get a serious job?* The question haunts me now and every time I claim unemployment, which the government has since rebranded as "reemployment," the friendlier face for collecting a handout.

Sitting in my car in the parking lot of a torn down building, I check my cracked iPhone screen to confirm I am at the correct location. Yep, this is it.

I get a text. It's Jacob.

Good luck beautiful. See you later.

Thanks babe. If you don't hear from me in an hour, you know what to do.

lol I have a feeling you're gonna be just fine.

God I look so young. Maybe if I put on glasses?

Stored in the center console for exactly these types of emergencies, I pull out my black-framed glasses hoping they will make me look older and more experienced. There. Now I look sophisticated.

After the agency finally went out of business, I quickly did the best thing I knew to do, find another job. It was a similar job title with a similar kind of agency, or so I thought. One month into that job I got myself fired. I say this because I literally stopped trying, a very uncharacteristic thing for me to do. It was the beginning of a different person I didn't recognize: the me who actually acted on my mental narrative.

I went to a top ten school for journalism and communication and then had a job that was exactly the perfect and desirable next step, a competitive position at an ad agency. I've always done the right thing until one day that became intolerable. I'd like to think it all unfolded as part of a plan set in motion by forces bigger than me. Or at least that's what I told myself when I got fired. That's what I'm telling myself now as I ride this creaky elevator up to my sketchy interview.

My last job, the one I pulled an Office Space at, was the used car lot of marketing agencies. A previous coworker set up the interview. They hired me immediately. My client was a liquid sugar company owned by a convicted cocaine dealer freshly out of prison. It seems he acquired the company through a deal he struck while behind bars. We were never clear on the how, but we were clear on his vision for branding the company as "the Tom's shoes of sugar," on account of his hiring mostly convicted felons to work there. We tried to explain this was slightly different, though I appreciated where his heart came from. He was giving these men a chance at a job and I thought that was nice. It was probably the only thing I found endearing about that experience.

One day, he stopped paying his bill. The CFO of the agency asked me, a newly hired account manager, to strong arm him into paying us by saying we were going to fire his entire team if not.

"Don't worry," he told me when he saw my eyes widen, "We're not. We just need to get him to pay us."

It became apparent to me we didn't have a contract, which was alarming. How does a serious company not sign a contract with their client before putting in a ton of hours and hiring someone who depended on that salary? Aren't there rules? It never occurred to me that maybe there aren't rules, that people can and often do whatever they want. Everyone at this strange company, including our client, was doing whatever they wanted. No one was following any rules and yet here I was trying to do exactly that.

I wish I could say that was the straw that broke the camel's back, but this was more of a slow burn. It took a few more bizarre events to invoke the guts to leave a perfectly good full-time gig. And by leaving, I mean stop working, keep showing up and wait until they politely tell me not to come back when they realize I'm not doing anything. To be honest, it took a surprisingly long time.

I should have known the first day I met the CEO of that company. He spoke like a car salesman from Jersey with food stuck in his teeth. Whatever he said sounded like he was chewing on a sandwich without noticing he was getting food everywhere. His meaty sausage hands were bloated, and his big pot belly poked out of the tight, bright shirts he wore, which strategically accentuated his every curve. He always wore gold chains that laid over an abundant bed of chest hair. He was shady Miami money and he was technically my boss.

We were in a conference room with the whole company and everyone stared at him in awe, laughing at bad jokes and trying to make eye contact. I was making a face like someone farted.

Anyway, the last straw that incited my lack of effort was when my immediate supervisor told me to embody Walmart. This was my second client, the one they moved me to when the sugar client finally admitted he would not be paying us anymore.

"You've got to Be Walmart," she said to me pounding her pale fists on the desk. She never took vacation days. Her hair was long, bleached and brittle. Her eyes were permanently droopy, and her skin was bloated from eating unhealthy leftovers at her desk every day. The effects of being Walmart for years. "Am I making sense?"

"Yes," I nodded, lying to her. People of Walmart photos flashed in my mind. Oh God. "May I be excused to the restroom, please?"

I quickly shut the door and flipped the lights on looking at myself in the mirror. Where are you? It was less of a question and more of an accusation.

Then, from the corner of my eye, I saw something sinister. WTF! It was a demon.

There was actually a life-size demon clown in the restroom.

It took me a moment to realize it was a Halloween prop the company produced for a theme park. They placed this thing directly in your line of vision on the toilet. A long deep breath is all I could let out as I finished peeing intently staring at the potty devil questioning my life's choices. Really, Cris? You wanna be Walmart? And that's the moment I gave up.

From then on, I would show up to work and do a number of things except my job, like online shopping, building a blog with my best friend, and texting Jacob all day. I knew it was bad. But my capacity for guilt momentarily turned off and I checked out. A month later I was fired.

Now, I'm wearing my black-framed glasses, which technically I don't really need as per the eye doctor who said I could probably do without them for a few more years. I insisted that one can never be too careful with their eyesight on account of the fact that I really wanted them.

Today, the elevator ride up to the fourth floor is creaky. The doors open and I step into a narrow hallway with ripped carpet, old doors and flickering lights, which I'm seeing in a slight blur that is just barely noticeable but there. I may actually be making my eyesight worse by wearing glasses and I don't have insurance anymore.

I should leave right now, but I won't. I need to go through this interview to make myself feel better, to make myself believe I'm trying to find a new job, to insist that I'm not defiantly flailing in the wind. The waiting room looks like the twilight zone. This is my last chance.

"Cris?"

Damn.

"Hello Cris," a man in a cheap brown suit says to me while motioning me to have a seat. He takes out a PowerPoint presentation, which he begins to read word-for-word making zero eye contact with me.

It's painful right from the get-go, and yet, I wonder where he got that suit. Who makes suits in this particular shade of pale brown? I can't quite place the color, but it's in the neighborhood of cat diarrhea. Yes, that's it. I knew I'd get it. It is the unmistakable shade of a loose cat stool.

"So, it sounds good to you?" he says, reacting to my smile.

"Uh, could you explain the role a bit more, with specifics?" I say, buying myself time to catch up.

As he describes the job to me—which is completely different from the posting—I put my hand up delicately and say, "I'm sorry, I don't believe this is a match. I'm not a salesperson."

"We have training," he quickly raises his voice in excited anticipation. Countless interviews just like this have prepared him for my objections. "In fact, what are your plans for the rest of the day? We can do a quick trial!"

My heart sinks. I've heard about these types of interviews. I am mortified this is happening to me. A handful of my good friends were bamboozled into interviews for marketing jobs that were really sales jobs in disguise, but this was when they were newbies applying fresh out of college. At the interview each one reported the same: they were essentially kidnapped into following people in their cars or worse, making cold calls for hours on a "trial."

"I need to be somewhere." I blurt out.

"Well, I have a side business, maybe you could help me with?" He points to another PowerPoint presentation conveniently pinned on the wall.

Jesus. I'm never leaving.

As he goes on to explain, I catch a bug crawling into my purse. A rage overtakes me as I realize what kind of bug this is. It's a fucking termite. For six months, we've had a termite problem that has been slowly chipping away at my sanity.

When Jacob and I made the big decision to get our own place together, a mere six months after dating, it was one of the most exciting times in my life... marred only by this. It started innocently as tiny piles of innocuous dust we discovered under our furniture. What's this? We scooped it up. It graduated to tiny wings discovered in the faucet, perhaps some sink flies? No worries. And then, one night, as Jacob and I finished decorating our brand-new cottage, we sat with the lights off to watch TV on the 60-inch flat screen that we sprung nearly $1,000 for. The screen began to turn black with little dots.

"That's odd," I said, grabbing the remote, "Maybe it's the setting?"

When technology could not solve the disappearing picture on the screen, we turned on the lights to discover in sheer terror that it wasn't a malfunction but an entire colony of winged creatures overtaking the TV. They were attracted to the glow and when we hit the lights, they began to fly all over the room.

Jacob would describe this as an inconvenience. I would describe this as the locusts in biblical times.

He frantically sprayed Raid and Windex to no avail, only a few of them were caught in the streaming liquid.

"Grab the Swiffer!" I screamed at him while swatting bugs.

He ran into our pantry, pulled out the swifter and one by one beat them to death. When it was done, we stood breathing deeply, adrenaline running through our veins still, my hair tousled, his shirt off, staring at a sea of murdered bug carcasses all over our freshly organized first home as a couple.

The problem didn't stop there. I implored our landlord, he didn't do much, I knew our exterminator by name. The experience also gave me a PhD in termites. As a side note and my personal pay-it-forward to you, here's the deal: don't inject your walls. It's a BS scam for money. Tent your house. Also, if you see a swarm, it means they've been in the house for as long as seven years laying eggs and waiting to mature so they can come out and fuck up your life.

Their swarming had become a nightly ritual. We planned our dinner around swarms, we kept a Swiffer out for when they did fly. It became an unhealthy obsession. I didn't sleep for fear they were in the beams above our bed. The cottage we chose made completely of wood changed from a charming, unique find to an all you can eat buffet for termites.

To see a termite crawling out of my bag during this interview is possibly the worst thing that could have happened. It is my personal hell, and still, because I am nothing if not polite, I suppress the shriek that wants to come out of my throat and instead begin swatting at my bag while trying to feign interest.

"How does that sound?" he says, interrupting my concentration.

"I'll call you."

Running out of the room with the mental image of a termite crawling all over my makeup laying eggs that will hatch in my eyes, I spill everything out onto the hallway floor until I find the thing. "Where are you?!" I scream to myself as people pass by. They all look suspicious, aimlessly strolling with files in hand, and yet I am the weirdo here. I have my personal belongings splattered on the faded carpet. I am the one sitting cross-legged in my nice clothes and sophisticated glasses frantically hunting a bug wondering what the hell I'm doing here.

Why am I trying so hard to do something different? I would never have taken this interview before. But I said yes because I've been saying yes to whoever will see me. I said yes because today, even though I don't have a way to earn an income, I can say I went out and tried.

The drive home goes by quick. I can't wait to pour myself a glass of wine. It's early. I don't care.

"In Europe this is normal," I say in my defense to no one. I am alone in our bug-infested home and now I'm talking to myself. There's no one to call, nothing to do. Jacob is at work. All my friends have jobs.

The first sip sends a bitter taste down my throat. Hot tears begin to come. I haven't cried this hard in a while and it feels like little pouches of water are popping in my eyes. Has my crying always been this excessive?

I take another sip hoping I'll be drunk soon since I haven't had breakfast. Then I start walking around the cottage, our first home together. It looks like something out of a magazine. The first day we signed the lease was the day the agency closed. I was worried that we wouldn't make the rent. Jacob insisted we would. We bought everything new and I had never done that before, neither had he. The couches are ours. The wine crates he nailed into the walls are ours. It's an entire home we designed together.

Well, except this. This lamp is only mine. My mother hates it. Jacob wasn't fond of it either. He tried to conveniently put it in the throw-away pile until I saw it, which only makes me like it more. I fought for this lamp, stubbornly. Its long silver base runs to about my thighs before it breaks out into two dozen plastic tendrils with tiny bulbs at the very end. It looks like a jellyfish that is admittedly out of sync with the design scheme. But I don't care that it stands out defiantly.

"I'll never let them toss you, my friend." I say as I play with its plastic appendages. Perhaps in some small way I am like this lamp, defiant and misplaced.

I'm starting to feel a buzz, so I move outside to the patio. It's a nice day out. The phone vibrates. It's Cassandra.

You good? Want to get a drink and talk about it?

Yes. Where?

***

Ambient sounds reach me from outside the cocktail bar. I can hear the steady drums of slow jamming music before I open the door to the rooftop bar. Gorgeous people walk in with their trendy outfits. The place is packed. Men in dark framed glasses and tight fitted blazers, women in leather skirts and gaudy jewelry and even androgynous looking figures float past us looking like magazine ads. This is not a place I feel comfortable in.

I begin to fidget with my purse. The day I don't wear heels and I go to the one bar in Miami where people are tall. None of them are from here. Real locals are mostly short. I feel normal amongst the average people in the city. Looking frantically for my friend, I go and sit by the bar hoping that my seated position will hide me.

"Hi friend," I say, finding Cassandra waiting for me. Thank god.

"How are you?" she says, sliding a drink towards me.

"I'm okay. I feel like a moth right now. Is this where all the pretty people in the city go?"

"It's cool, huh?"

She is at ease looking around and swinging to the trendy elevator music. I envy her ability to blend in any environment. I'm not as socially versatile. Right now, though shorter than all the lanky modelesque bodies around us, she is radiant. I am looking nervously hoping I don't have to pee because then I'd have to get up and politely excuse myself by tapping on

139

everyone's waistline.

"Yeah. Super."

"So, talk to me, how are you doing?" she asks, clasping her cocktail and eyeing the bar. She's scanning for potential.

"Well, I spent the day drinking wine. I haven't eaten anything but a Pop Tart and my own tears. Unemployment doesn't suit me quite yet. Excuse me, reemployment."

"Reemployment?"

"That's what they call it now. It's been rebranded."

"Oh, I see," she says, giggling. "You'll be fine. I'm not worried about you. Embrace the fucking pause. It's a gift, a little wrinkle in time when you get to do you." She takes another sip.

"I don't know how to take a pause. Or I guess, I don't know how not to 'work.' I never felt exactly happy at my job but for a moment there I felt like I was doing what I should be doing."

"I hear you. But that's bullshit," she says tartly. She's on the verge of dropping out of her PhD program. I know this and I know this is affecting her advice. But maybe that's not such a bad thing.

"Are you dropping out?"

"Yes," she says, putting her drink down smiling. "I think so."

"What will you do?" I immediately take on her situation as my own forgetting about me and now dutifully concerned about her future. "What about your mom? What about all that time and money in the program?"

She confidently changes her stance. "I have a master's degree so it's not like an incomplete doctorate. And I just can't do it right now. I need to change it up. I need new energy."

"Okay then." Sometimes I don't exactly know what she means. Either she can't articulate it or doesn't want to. I also know when it's time to stop pressing. This is a time to drop it. "How's that guy you were dating?"

I honestly can't remember his name. I didn't think he'd stick around for that long, so I didn't bother to learn it.

"Well, you know," she says, sipping her cocktail. "He's there.

I..." she trails off. I know what this means. She's thinking of the details, but she will tell me a few sentences rich with vagueness. "We're evolving with each other and acclimating to our need for space. It's all a process but I may call him later. Who knows?"

She immediately turns her body around and sweeps the room with her big brown eyes and wavy dark hair.

I keep sipping my drink wishing to be invisible and trying not to focus on the fact that it's probably an $18 cocktail. "I think I may go soon."

"Why?" she says, quickly popping her body around.

"I dunno. I probably shouldn't be out spending money right now."

"This is the best time to be out spending money," she says smiling. "You don't have to go to work tomorrow. You can wake up and worry about applying for a job later, which no doubt will be easy for you."

She says this matter-of-factly, but she's subtly letting on that she thinks finding another traditional job is an obvious choice. It's the easy choice and there's plenty of hamster wheels to crawl into. She's right. Staying unemployed while finding out what I really want to do would be more difficult for me. Finally finishing the book I started and committing to that life is the harder choice. Springing on the expensive cocktail and then getting another safe job is easy, and she's right, it'll be waiting for me in the morning.

"Okay, fuck it. I'll stay," I say, leaning back and trying to relax. I can decide which direction to take tomorrow. "Jesus, everyone here is so tall and perfect."

"I know. Enjoy the view, friend," she says, taking her glass to mine.

13
Show me yours, I'll show you mine

The first few months of our romance, Jacob and I felt like new parents with a good first child, boastful about how easy it all is when you know what you're doing, never mind the sleepless nights of the second kid that are well on their way.

Oh, you fight? Sigh. Wow, I guess we really don't. We're just, you know, so in love.

Then time passed and reality set in. Relationships, even the most healthy ones, are hard. Who knew? I had been preparing myself for years to be in love, never thinking there would be work to do after the fact. As naive as it sounds, the notion that even the best relationships take work stunned me. For as many subjects as Jacob and I were on the same page about, there were fundamental beliefs we dissented on. These seeds of disagreement would grow into the most painful parts of understanding who we are together, or more importantly, who I am with Jacob.

The story and the work is far from over after you find your person and throw a fistful of celebratory confetti.

Being single and focused on who I was made me an overachiever prepared to go into a relationship like a straight-A student. I knew myself fully. I had a thoughtful answer for every question, until it was an equation that involved taking his feelings into account. The complexities of starting a life with him crept up on me and all of a sudden, the beliefs I felt were absolute began to turn wishy-washy. I found myself repeating the banal sayings I'd heard women repeat before me to friends that judged them: It's not so simple, or you don't know unless you're in it.

It tastes bad now as I say it while I pace around our home with every piece of me so anxious, I can't even sit down. Jacob and I just got into a monster fight. I pick up my phone and call him. He doesn't answer. Although every logical part of me knows this is a fight and it'll blow over, a primal uncontrollable feeling kicks me in the gut. What if this time he doesn't come back? What if this is the fight that does us in?

I run to the bathroom because I think I'm going to be sick.

What if he leaves me? What am I supposed to do?

A highlight reel of all my most embarrassing, stupid life choices begins to play as my arms slump over the toilet. I don't feel like I can control it. It's the thing that makes my imagination a horrible place of self-inflicted cruelty.

I see all the people who would take sickening pleasure if we were to break up with vivid clarity. First, I imagine my parents, though not happy for the breakup because they have grown to love Jacob, would certainly somehow mention how disappointed they were that we moved in before getting married. You know the saying, *Lo que empieza mal, acaba mal... what starts bad, ends badly.* Then, of course, in perfect order a list of the friends I no longer speak to join the party. They disapprovingly cackle amongst each other, well we knew that wouldn't last. I save the best for last, his ex-girlfriend, happy as can be to finally win the battle in claiming her stake on his heart, *oh you thought you two would, like, end up together? LOL.*

My elbows begin to ache, and this position hurts my back, a reminder that I'm approaching my thirties. How can this be happening? I get up to wash my face and look in the mirror. Like an alcoholic who has spent years in rehabilitation, I shake my head wondering how I'm relapsing right now. I went to therapy, I spent time alone, I've read all the books, I've done all the work.

I must be depressed, or worse, have real problems. Painful problems that no one can solve, not even Jacob, who is mostly a perfect partner except when he can be a real shithead and walk out of our front door in the middle of an argument.

Come to think of it, I put up with a lot! I don't have to take this. You know how many self-help books I've read so I can be fair and considerate during our arguments? I didn't get up and leave like a Goddamn child. I'm packing a bag.

Blow dryer, extra underwear, jeans, comfortable shoes. That should be fine.

Is this a bad idea? NO! Every second you stay here you lose! *LEAVE!* my gut screams, but I can't seem to get rid of a calm voice that's barely noticeable in the background of my mental choir... Hey you, the voice says casually, maybe responding to bad behavior with bad behavior won't work because then you'll create... more bad behavior.

I consider it for a moment. Nope, that sounds ridiculous. My hands are shaking, and I call Cassandra. It's the only reasonable thing I can think of doing.

"Hey," I say, my voice cracks holding back tears.

"What's wrong, my friend?" she says sweetly on the line.

"I got into a fight with Jacob. He left and now he won't pick up. So, I wanna leave. I don't wanna be here waiting for him. I'm going crazy, I think."

"Cris, you're always welcome here, but I think it's better if you stay. Leaving sets a precedent in your relationship that can't be taken back."

"But he walked out! I don't even know where he is. WHY ARE YOU BEING SO CALM, CASSANDRA?"

"I know. He shouldn't have done that, but he's probably coming right back and it's better for you to be there. Sometimes guys need to walk away for a minute."

We hang up and I pace. I put the bag down and pour myself a glass of wine. Probably not the best decision I can be making but I need something in my hands. You know? Fuck him. I'm going for a walk. Why not? I refuse to be here waiting for him. If by the time I'm finished he's not back, I'm leaving with my bag.

I pour my wine into a to-go cup so the couples in matching tracksuits who frequently walk their dogs in Coconut Grove won't judge me. Sure enough, as soon as I walk out the door, there's a man jogging who nods hello followed by a couple having a nice conversation as they walk their black lab. I nod trying to hide my to-go cup. Crap, what am I even wearing? Leggings, my baggy college sweater and Uggs? Miami is breezy but hardly for this attire. Whatever, I need to move.

My body is trembling from my nerves. I make my way down the sidewalk of our busy street and turn to go into a neighborhood where there's more privacy. That way all the people with healthy habits and relationships will not take pity on my drinking alone in the streets. As I make the turn towards my safety street, a figure steps out of the darkness. It's Jacob.

"Hey," he says, sounding a bit resigned.

"Hi." Really, hey? Just hey? Like you're not abandoning me. OK, hey guy.

"Look I'm sorry. About this. Everything. It's such a stupid fight and I love you so much. You're my whole world and nothing is ever going to matter that much. I just needed to cool down is all."

My body is still shaking again but this time thinking of my foolishness. I acted like such a child, when all I needed to do was... calm down and wait. Give him his breathing room. Instead, I made a huge mess. I'm so embarrassed I start to cry.

"Babe, why are you crying? It's okay." Jacob says, coming closer to hug me.

"Please don't leave like that ever again," I say.

We walk back to our cottage together and just like that

become part of the healthy relationship walkers in our neighborhood.

Jacob is the only person I've confessed everything to. He is my friend in the whole sense of that word, the best I've ever had. And best friends deserve our honesty. So, when we get back and he sees my bag by the door, I tell him to sit.

"When you walk out in the middle of a fight without telling me you'll be back, I get scared. In fact, I got so scared and mad, I packed a bag with the intention of leaving. I imagined all kinds of frankly embarrassing things, like all the people who will one day dance on my grave celebrating the fact that we broke up."

I begin to fidget with my hands and Jacob stops me.

"There's more. I'm deeply scared you'll leave me." I explain to him like we're in a confessional.

It feels like stomach-lava to have these thoughts pour out of my mind and onto our living room floor, and yet, it oddly feels like a power has been stripped away from them. Actually, it feels like an elephant just took its foot off my chest and I can breathe. These are the things I've fought so hard to hide because what self-respecting man won't leave you if he finds out you're terrified he will? Being so in love it makes you desperate is not sexy, it goes against all the advice I've ever gotten.

I'd never want anyone to know these are the things I think of when no one's looking, least of all Jacob— not to mention he is the least drama-ridden person I know and wholly unconcerned with the opinions of others. It's shameful that deep down I'm insecure and my faith in myself is a fragile thing I need to tend to on a daily basis. Every time the feelings come, I mask them with positive, self-affirming thoughts and pretend they never happened.

Jacob gets weepy eyed. It's a sight I've literally never seen. They're not tears yet, but I can see his blood shot eyes and that glossy layer that tears make right before they blur your vision and squeeze themselves right out.

He presses me closely and squeezes me harder than usual.

"Nothing you ever think will make me stop loving you. I love you more than anything and anyone. And I'll never leave you, I promise you. Please don't ever be embarrassed to show me who you are. I've got my fears too, like one day you might discover someone else could give you a better life and you'll leave me. I get scared that you'll tire of my mood swings, that I'm not the best man for you after all."

"What? God, you're the one that's supported me the last few years while I figure out my job, my book, my life," I say, still in shock he has these feelings too.

I never realized how isolated I am in the moments of my negative thoughts. It's elementary, but I forget we're all human and we all experience the same feelings of fear and inadequacy, of not enoughness. When I'm spiraling in a shame storm, I always feel like I'm alone, like everyone else has their shit together or at the very least has far less self-induced drama than I do. But even Jacob, a guy that cares nothing about what others think, has his own shame and insecurity. We really aren't alone. None of us are.

**

The next morning things are calmer. I decided to take a mental health day. Jacob has left for work and I have our cabin all to myself. We're leaving for Spain soon, anyway, so maybe I'll even do the laundry, pull out our bags and pack. We'll see. This is my refuge and the only way I know how to process things, at the keyboard. Luckily for me, Jacob is well acquainted with the life of someone dating a writer. He gave me his blessing long ago to derive whatever inspiration necessary from our relationship. I never take that privilege lightly, writing is my vocation, it is a gift always meant to do good, to express something and leave the world a little lighter because of it, never ever to point the finger or blame.

I've just reheated my coffee and settled in to do some writing.

Although I have a desk in our guest room, my best writing often happens right here on the couch. I sit cross legged, plop a pillow on my lap and set my laptop right on top. Where do I begin?

Showing the ugly parts of me is the most important thing I've ever done in my relationship. In fact, I've only ever been this honest about who I am and how I feel with Jacob. I was always so scared of revealing that to anyone else because I thought men wanted mystery, to feel like the threat of a woman leaving them at any moment is real because, you know, that's what really keeps them interested. And that role is exhausting.

The second most important thing I did for my relationship with Jacob is heed this fundamentally vital piece of advice: Do not sit back and expect someone else to make things happen for you. Go create those things yourself.

At the beginning of our relationship, I wanted certain things I wasn't sure how to ask for. I was used to hoping and wishing, that if I could hint at these things, Jacob would catch onto them and give them to me. Busting out of "Rapunzel culture" is one of the hardest kinds of self-work I've done. The hard part wasn't switching my actions, although for a while it went against my every instinct, it was the constant bad advice and judgement I got from other people still playing life by those rules.

I was taught that I am a princess, but not just any princess, I am a princess so out of reach that I live in an ivory tower. My love can only be made available to the most persistent, determined suitors who must literally wear themselves to the point of exhaustion in a setup that's design is futile by nature...all so they can have the chance to reach me.

If I recall the story correctly, eventually Rapunzel let her hair down because she is in charge of her own happiness. This is not a memo I grew up with. This damsel-in-distress thing is ingrained into Hispanic girls from birth.

I take another sip of my coffee. Shit, cold already. I hate having to get up and reheat it when I'm in a groove. I impatiently wait for the microwave to let me know my coffee is now warm and make my way back into my writing position. Where was I...

Why am I thinking of this now? Well, my crusade of self-understanding led me to widen the scope on where to search for the answer to the question I've been asking myself throughout my twenties: Why am I the way I am?

Culture, it turns out, is a key indicator.

Hispanic culture in Miami is amazing and rich with so many positive nuances. However, when it comes to being a woman or man, we pretty much have these highlights to look forward to: male bravado, fetishized jealousy and traditionally inconvenient gender roles. There's a reason Miami is surprisingly filled with red voters: we can be the lesser known mirror of the Bible Belt, traditionally repressive in a lot of the same ways.

Things are changing, but make no mistake, the roots of being raised in that climate made me a traditionally repressed, goody two-shoes for the formative years of my life. Going away to college was a playground for my self-development. Gainesville was completely different from Miami, it felt like a neutral place where I could explore all kinds of beliefs, values, even religions, often trying them on for a week or more to see how they fit. What came out was not exactly a finished product, but I was indeed changed in some fundamental ways.

That didn't mean the old beliefs went away easily. No, when something is that far ingrained in us, it lingers in an unconscious way for a long time. When I moved back to Miami and began dating men exclusively from a genetic pool of people raised to play into these rules, it was an entirely new obstacle to overcome.

When I committed to Jacob, I was unwilling to play those games anymore. If I want trust, I am to trust. If I want affection, I am to be affectionate. If I want unconditional love with radically open communication, I am to give all those things freely and without cost. Give without expecting.

Since the beginning, I've laid it all out for Jacob. It's not that it came easily, it didn't. I was so fed up and greatly impatient with playing games that I took every opportunity to let him know exactly how I felt. Not because I'm fearless, dear God no, but because I feel as if I'm running out of time here. My thought process when we began dating was: if this kinda shit scares you now, run.

"Hey, you went on that business trip and you only called me once that day. That won't work. I like being called in the morning, throughout the day and at night before bed. If that kinda thing is overly needy, you're free to let me know if you don't think that'll work for you. But that's what I want if you wanna keep dating me," I said to him after his first business trip. He'd forgotten to call me a number of times and I felt like days went by since we spoke. I realized after the third day how irritated I was, so I told him flat out. It was highly outside of my character at the time.

"Wow," he said, dazed that I put it so matter-of-factly. "Yeah, I can do that, not a problem. Sorry, I'm just not used to that, but I'd love to talk to you more."

That one interaction would have been months of getting mad and being passive aggressive in hopes my previous suitor would finally get it. It was highly impractical, so I figured I'd skip ahead to the end with Jacob because if I can't get something as basic as the number of phone calls I want, what are we doing here?

To my surprise, Jacob liked this. It was such a shock I wondered if I should tell the others. Starting with my friends and then moving on to every woman I've ever found crying in the bathroom at a bar: Hey, stop what you're doing and listen to me. If you simply ask for what you want in plain English, you'll get it. That's all. Stop reading all this crappy advice in blogs. If the first few dudes don't respond to your requests, better to weed them out early on and get to the one that eventually will agree that what you want is reasonable and, hey, they like you.

This part is simple and clear cut. Now, forming a relationship and redefining who you are together, well unfortunately, there's no simple strategy there. You get to put in the work. That's all. So really like the person you pick to do the work with because sometimes the work tastes like shit.

It's one of the greatest gifts to really see another person. I see Jacob. He sees me. We've had many conversations in a room with our ugliness sitting right next to us, now expectant puppies to their owners. Because that is exactly what both our deepest fears have turned into after speaking them out loud. Our shame over time has converted into nothing but mere pups wagging their tails as we train them not to pee on the carpet, all the while letting them know they are loved no matter how much urine we have to clean. They'll get it eventually.

14

A new beginning

I'm on a couch in Madrid, Spain feverishly text-messaging my sister. Jacob went out for a walk with his mom, leaving me here in her apartment to sit with my thoughts. Marriage is on my mind. I hate that it is, but I can't ignore it. I love and hate traveling for this reason, it provides a removal and necessary space for everything underneath the surface to bubble up. All the nagging thoughts I strategically put at bay in my regular life all of a sudden crash into my consciousness when I'm outside of my usual environment.

Our trip over was good. I was excited to get away, change scenery and come back to Spain. It's been so long since my last visit, which was during those college years when life looked completely different. Now I'm living with Jacob, the guy who took us to a hookah bar, meeting his family and yearning for him to propose. His family here is wonderful and it all fits in a way it never quite has. They care about me, I can tell, so what's missing?

A reply comes back to me in broken international text-messaging. Sofi tells me not to spoil a good trip in the city we met in.

This isn't the time to bring that up. It's obvious you love each other, so be in Spain for now. Enjoy that!

It's notably softer in tone than usual, but nevertheless, I can't shake it off. I've feigned that marriage isn't important to me for a long time, when in fact it is. The more I deny it, the more it nips at my heels. I have a process for understanding subjects. It's not unlike what I do before I write something. I try to wrap my head around what it means to me before I start putting pen to paper. If I simply begin following a whim, I won't finish and it'll get stuffed somewhere unused in my various notebooks.

So I did my part to understand marriage. I read books and articles detailing the history of this sanctity. I read personal essays on the subject. I even asked several married friends what they think about it. The feedback was mixed.

"Something changes, for sure," one friend told me, though she could not put her finger on what exactly.

"Oh gosh, once you've lived together, it's all the same," another friend said.

Originally, marriage was an arrangement based on mutual gain, usually financial. It's only in the last century that the idea of marriage became based on love. This was from one of the books I read. The author didn't make a compelling case for marriage. In his view, the institution began for its originally intended purpose (money, land and social status) and only got warped in the last hundred years, a model which hasn't proven to work well, if we're looking at the divorce statistics.

I feared my research wasn't helping because everything that came up on the subject seemed to point to one conclusion: it's all relative. I hate those words. It's all relative is a cop out for people who don't want to take a position and be wrong, so they skirt out of things by saying, "Well it's all relative." And yet, that's where my research pointed.

In the end, peeling away everything outside of facts, my takeaway is this: it is most definitely the worst contract you can ever enter into. There are zero guarantees. It can have huge financial implications. It is a legal formality that in no way binds two people forever. Also, the numbers don't look good.

And yet still, I want it.

I don't want to be the type of girl who wants a ring. I want to be the type of woman who doesn't need that, who doesn't want a relationship structure that can be traditional and repressive, maybe even dated. Accepting and owning that this is important to me is one of the hardest pills to swallow. It did not go down easily.

So, I turned my attention to the people who were pro-marriage, my tribe, much as I did not want to admit it. I sifted through a lot of answers, most of which I threw away immediately. The pro-marriage folks did not have as thoughtful or compelling arguments in favor of the institution as the anti-marriage people. That much was obvious from the start. It took a while of searching, while feeling defeated that this was my clan, until I found something beautiful.

No contract keeps two people together. Our commitment to each other does that. The invisible acts of love we bring to the table every day do that. The accepting and even liking our most obvious character flaws does that. Our choice to act from a higher place than feelings, which come and go, does that. These are the things that make people chosen family. These are the things parents and friends don't see when they ask when you're going to be engaged, because it's been a while, you know?

I delete the text messages between my sister and I. It's not because Jacob will see, he's not the kind of boyfriend who checks my phone. It's for me, so I don't have to be reminded of what I want and don't have, of being that girl.

"Hey!" Jacob calls from the small foyer, he's got a few bags.

"Hey babe. How was your walk?"

"Awesome," he says, grinning. "Are you ready to take a drive to Toledo? I can't wait to show you this city in a new way."

"Hell yeah," I say, already stuffing it down. It's working. "Should I get our bag?"

"Yeah, pack light. We can stay at my aunt's place. She lives nearby."

***

Toledo is one of Jacob's favorite cities in Spain. His aunts live in Nambroca, a nearby town, and he spent his childhood summers in Cuerva, another town not too far from here. I've been to Toledo with my parents, but it was before I could drink so in my mind that simply doesn't count. My own personal travel theory: if you can't visit the bars of a city, you haven't gotten to know its pulse. For all intents and purposes, this was my first visit to Toledo.

A medieval city with mixed architecture reveals itself as our tiny European car makes its way across a draw bridge over what appears to be a moat. I can't help but liken it to Game of Thrones, an observation that makes me feel terribly uncultured. There are Arabian arches mixed with Roman architecture and the cobblestone streets that are Spain's signature foundation. Toledo was Spain's original capital, a fact Jacob happily shared with me along the way. I skillfully took out my phone and wrote myself a message to look that up without him noticing.

My education in geography and history have been a source of embarrassment over the past few years. Namely, my realizing that I either didn't pay attention or care enough to remember much. What do I recall from those years? Having crushes on boys, training bras and the five models of hair irons my mother bought me in high school before I found the right one for my hair type. Unfortunately, the world map and significant historical events just didn't make the cut.

Jacob doesn't care, in fact, just a few days ago on the way over to Spain, we took an edible before our flight. It was a long one, so we figured, why not?

"Africa isn't a country?" I said to him, so stoned I could barely move my limbs.

"Babe," he said, laughing so hard he was crying. "No, no it's not."

I was worried that I wouldn't be able to get onto the airplane, but an entirely new worry took its place as I mentally scanned for all the potential times I referred to Africa as a country over my lifetime.

"Fuck," I said. "What... never mind."

"Go ahead, ask me it's fine."

"No, you're gonna laugh at me and I can't feel my face."

He did manage to convince me to ask eventually and then he graciously educated me on Africa, but I vowed I'd use Google as a first resort.

"You know, this city is renowned for its ethnic and religious diversity?" I said, trying to read the tiny letters on my screen.

"I do," he said while maneuvering our car into the tiniest parking spot I have ever seen. "What's wrong?"

"I can't look," I said, burying my face.

"*Ayyy mi amor*," he said, laughing. "I'm done, you can open your eyes now."

Traditional Spanish restaurants and Hookah bars line the very narrow streets. It all seems like it shouldn't go together, and yet it works.

"Let's grab a quick glass of wine?" Jacob says, putting the parking ticket in his pocket and counting some euros.

"Yes please," I say, smelling the fresh marzipan from a bakery we pass, it's one of many here that make this signature pastry. "God that smells good."

"Here!" he says, taking my arm abruptly and walking inside a tiny bar I would have passed without noticing.

I like places like this, a hidden quality is typically the sign of a good time, which happens to be Jacob's specialty. He is a world traveler in his heart. He's street smart, a natural ability I envy, but also just has a nose for a good time. With a quick Google, or even a few guesses based on instinct and little more, Jacob will take us to the best secret spot in any town, whether he's been there or not.

He directs me to a small bench and goes to order from the bar. The place can't be bigger than our cottage living room, which is to say it's quite small. American jazz music is playing and it catches my ear immediately. It's quite an unusual background melody here. I often tease Jacob because the only music they play in Spain is techno or songs from the nineties. The floors are an elegant marble and there is a big mirror with lists of all the cocktails they make. The walls behind me are lined with black and white photos of patrons from over the years.

"Here you go," he says, handing me a glass of red wine. I can already tell it's going to be good. It smells tart and earthy.

"Why thank you," I say, taking my first sip. "It's perfect. This place is perfect. How did you find it?"

"Ahh, it's a highly cultivated skill, really."

"I am truly impressed."

The server brings us a small bowl of Spanish olives.

"Gracias," he says. "Try one."

"Oh no, I don't like olives. You go ahead."

"Come on," he says, pinching into one and bringing it to my mouth. "Just one."

I grab it from his hand and hold it, no part of me wanting to stick this thing in my mouth. I already know I don't like olives.

"You know, my mom didn't like olives for years and then one day her uncle made her eat nine in a row. That's what it took. Now she likes them," I say, my face twisting a bit grotesquely still staring at the olive.

Jacob laughs. "Well, that's one way to do it."

"I suppose it is. Fuck it, why not?" I said, popping the whole thing into my mouth. It's chewy from the start, but after a while something happens, something good. The salty, oily flavors actually taste all right with the wine.

"You like it, don't you?" he says, he hasn't stopped looking at me.

"Okay, fine. I actually kind of like this one. They taste

different though, right?"

It's my way of not letting him be completely right.

"They do," he says, popping an olive into his mouth and washing it down with wine. "I'm glad you like them. It wouldn't be right to be Spanish and not like the olives here."

I've spent years under the pretense that I don't like olives. If I can be the person who likes olives though, what other kind of person can I be? All of a sudden the olive incident opens up a world of possibilities. Maybe I could be anti-marriage. That would be very European of me.

We pay our bill after a second round and walk the streets, buzzing on wine at this point. All my worries about marriage and a weak history foundation fade away. I can't tell if it's the wine or my newfound persona. I don't care. I feel better. If this is love, maybe I don't actually want to be married. Maybe we will be like Kurt Russell and Goldie Hawn and our relationship will stand the test of time, laughing in the face of the institution. I'm not a trained monkey that can't think for itself. If I can't rationalize why marriage is important to me then this is obviously coded into my brain by society. And I am better than that. We will show the world our love.

"Jacob?" I say, looking around for him. But Jacob is gone.

He's standing inside someone's house, well actually their patio. Many of the houses in this city are built around their patio, I learned in my earlier Google search. The outdoor area is central to the home. You can't see someone's patio unless the front door is open, which it is right now.

Jacob is talking to a man, who I can only imagine is asking him why the hell he walked into his home. He waves at me to come inside, but I refuse on account of his tendency to make friends with strangers, and I'm not in the mood to make small talk. I am having an epiphany, goddamnit.

"It's cool, I know him. We're staying here for the night."

"What?"

"Surprise!" He says beaming. His smile is childlike in its

enthusiasm and he's raising his arms inside the center square of what is honestly the most beautiful historical Toledan home I have ever seen. It even has Spanish moss on the stone walls.

"Beg your pardon?"

"We have dinner plans tonight, so let's get our luggage and get ready."

***

Dinner is tapas at La Malquerida, another place Jacob can be proud of choosing. If I was a restaurant, I would be this one. The colors are the first thing I notice. Bright bursts of pinks and greens pop among the neutral beiges. There are little knick knacks everywhere but not enough to be kitschy, it's still clean. My favorite part is where we are currently seated, a small section that looks like a cozy living room with a few couches, a coffee table and a library of books. To our right are big windows facing all the traffic walking Toledo's streets. A peak people watching position.

"I gotta hand it to you. You've outdone yourself again. How did you find this?" I say eating a croqueta so delicious I never want the flavor of anything else in my mouth ever again.

"A master never reveals his secrets," Jacob says, he winks and then goes to order us a round of drinks.

"La Malquerida," I say, reading the menu out loud. It means a girl who is not loved right, someone who has had bad luck in love. Now that is interesting.

"You know," he says, interrupting my thoughts. "I've always wanted a relationship like my grandparents. I really love that my grandpa has served my grandma coffee and an English muffin in bed every morning for fifty years. I want to be like that with you. I think we already are like them."

He slides a giant gin and tonic towards me.

"I love that too."

I heard stories about his grandparents before I met them.

160

Austin and Lucy lived in a house made of granite on the side of a mountain overlooking a small town in The Smokies. When I met them for the first time, I saw for myself their sweet routine. Jacob and Lucy are both sleepers. I am an early bird, so every morning I'd get up and sure enough, Austin had made a fresh batch of coffee. He happily poured me a cup.

"Good morning kiddo," he said, handing me the cup and continuing to finish making sausages and toasting English muffins. He had this formula down to the minute; I could tell it gave him a sense of pride. He is as methodical as he is intelligent, and even in this sweet endeavor, I saw how his brain worked. He got the sausage just right so he could time it perfectly and wake Lucy up with breakfast in bed. It was a daily act of love so touching it would melt the most cynical of hearts. A strong case for the pro-marriage team.

"So listen, we have an early day tomorrow," Jacob says.

"Really? We never get up early. I feel like we're passed that point," I said, giggling.

"Nah, we'll be fine. Trust me, it'll be worth it. When do I ever let you down? Cheers!"

He brings his giant gin and tonic to mine and it makes a clink sound. The gin and tonics here are served in something resembling a fishbowl. I have to hold mine with both hands.

"The gin tonics here are really something, huh?"

"They just don't make them the same anywhere else, trust me. I've been to over twenty countries and no one else gets it right," Jacob says stirring his giant cocktail with a straw that is comically small.

"Spaniards are all the same," I say, laughing. "Nothing is as good as it is in Spain."

"We're not all like that," he says playfully. "And besides, it's true."

But they are all like that, a fact I don't mind. I think it's true too, but then again my family is from here so it's obvious which side of the debate I'd land on. On our way into Spain, thankfully hours after the edibles wore off, Jacob strategically got into the line for European passports entering the country, a much shorter line. He can do this on account of having both an American and Spanish passport. He presented both to the man at the booth, who looked bored and like he took his job as seriously as most Spaniards, which is to say, not seriously at all.

When he saw both passports slide towards him, he swatted the American one away like a pest.

"No," he said, looking directly at Jacob in the eyes. "*Usted, Español.*" He rolled the pronunciation extra to make his point.

I handed him my American passport apologetically hunching my shoulders as if to say, well, these things do happen.

Jacob quickly explained, "Ella es mi novia Americana." She's my American girlfriend.

The man didn't look at me but gave Jacob a face. It was as if he said: I'm sorry dude. I wanted to clarify that I too was Spanish, but we were scooted off too soon.

Anyway, a real Spaniard doesn't get up before 10 AM so I'm counting on Jacob's genes to get out of our plans tomorrow. He'll probably snooze anyway. I say this to myself as I finish my goblet of gin and we walk out, holding hands and kissing in the streets.

Everything is wet for some reason, though it hasn't rained. Perhaps someone cleaned it? It doesn't matter. The cobblestone sparkles and the city at this time of night is magic. Crowds of young people pass us by. I can't believe how many people are out at this time. I smell smoke from the small groups gathered outside bars, food from the restaurants that are remarkably serving people at 12 AM, and something else mixed in I can't really describe. It's a scent specific to Spanish air. I don't know what it is but it smells like this everywhere. I take a deep breath hoping to capture it. They say some of the most vivid recollections can linger in your olfactory memory.

Somehow, we make it to our Toledan house in several twists and turns down narrow streets that all look the same to me.

Thank God Jacob pays attention or has that special directional antenna. Back in our room, we make love with all the intensity of two people drunk on gin and good conversation. He even lets me go to bed with the bathroom light on so I can see the beams shine through the large intricate wooden doors with an Arabian design. The room is filled with tiny stars. It's these specks of light that are the last thing I remember before falling sound asleep.

***

At 8 AM I fight a raging hangover and my curly hair. It turns out for the first, and only, time ever in our four and a half years together, Jacob is up and ready to make the most of the day. I stand in front of the mirror trying to do something with this mop of waves that doesn't want to cooperate.

"I need coffee," he says all upbeat.

"Okay, I need Sprite and Advil. And a minute."

I stumble around bumping into the stool and forgetting what I should be doing, so he helps me pack our things and directs me to my clothes. This is the roughest morning I've had in a long time. Remarkably, we make our way slowly to a coffee shop nearby. Everything is dead this early. I'm so cranky.

Jacob orders us two espressos and we take a seat.

"We're going to see this amazing trail," he says, sliding my coffee towards me and looking up something on his phone. The telltale sign he's found some place worth visiting.

My insides are still arguing with being vertical. Everything about a park right now feels stupid. I nod at him, accepting my fate. He's like a dog with a bone this morning, so I don't argue. I'm already here.

We walk outside and I take note that not one Spaniard is awake or out. Only Asian tourists are walking the streets on guided tours and us, two people who should be sleeping off our hangovers. The fresh air helps.

"It's right over here," he says, and we make our way to a path along the Tagus River, which wraps around Toledo's old town.

Something about his insistence makes me think there's a reason we're doing this, but I don't allow my mind to go there. I'm suddenly grateful for my hangover which is becoming a welcome distraction. The last time Jacob orchestrated a surprise and acted weird about it, I thought he was proposing. It was Christmas time and we were in our cottage. He told me to wait in the room while he set everything up. I stayed in there for an hour and a half, which was plenty of time to come out to rose petals and an elaborate romantic setup. Instead, when I came out there was Jacob smiling with a bicycle. I only ever used the thing once and then it got stolen. A part of me believes it never stood a chance.

Anyway, none of that matters now that marriage is out. I've come too far. The walk is pebbly, and the colors are stunning. If I had more energy, I'd take photos. The toasty oranges of the earth meet the varying blues of the river and sky. There isn't a soul out on the trail, it's just us. The sound of our boots is all we hear besides the water flowing and an occasional bird above us.

"Let's take a photo." He says, so I begin to pose for a selfie with him in the sun. "No, no I'll set up the camera over there and get us with the background."

"Really?" I say, looking around. The view is stunning, no doubt, but if we take a selfie we strategically avoid the elaborate, albeit beautiful, birdcage that's covered in shit. The smell makes me slightly nauseous.

"Don't worry, I'll make sure we don't get it. Go stand over there."

Ever so often the scent of bird poop wafts in the river's breeze right to this very spot, but I do as I'm told, covering my wavy hair with a hat. Hopefully, that looks good. I've got no way to tell.

He makes his way up and grabs my arm to face the camera. As I try to fix my hair under the hat one more time, he bends down on one knee. The photo snaps. I remain here oddly in shock.

"Will you marry me?" he said.

"Really?" I say, it's all I can manage to get out.

"Yeah, really! Well?"

"Yes," I say. "Don't get up yet. I want to keep a photo of this moment in my mind."

And just like that I joined team marriage once again. Did I experience flashbacks to all the little moments that made this one special? Not really. But I feel butterflies in my stomach and the stirrings of something beautifully indescribable in my heart. My logical side has been analyzing marriage for the better part of the trip and there simply is no logic to explain this bliss. I am smiling so hard I think my cheekbones are going to hurt tomorrow.

I am experiencing freedom and clarity, and I want to hold on to it, but I fear it only ever visits me in brief moments before it escapes. I don't have to understand or work so hard to rationalize my feelings. Sometimes, desire exists outside of all the arguments for or against it. I want to marry this man, the man who would surprise me and drag me out of bed early just so I could be proposed to on a trail with a million-dollar view of the Tagus River.

The diamond shimmers blue from the reflection of the sky— because the clouds parted on this January morning after weeks of gray to deliver a day in Spain that rightfully belongs in May.

"I had several nightmares you'd hate this ring," he says right away. "Do you like it?"

"I do," I say, and I really mean it, though I honestly don't think I'd care what it looks like. It was never about the actual ring.

I take another mental photo of Toledo's rolling hills, all the remarkable rock formations that took years to manifest into a view that inspires awe. I etch in my mind the Tagus River cascading in a flowing blue. It's been running through Toledo for centuries and I get to see it right now with Jacob. It's all right here, right down to the elaborate antique birdcage covered in crap. It's the most perfect thing I'll ever see.

"Let's keep going," he says, holding my hand and leading me through the trail. We do it in silence, the same comfortable silence that's always existed between us.

Of all the ways of looking at marriage, I think one of the simplest ways to see it is a choice. Every day we walk around making choices. We are decision-making machines, whether we realize it or not. I've shied away from making decisions but even that avoidance is a decision. We have the choice to do whatever we please with whomever we please. Choice is a fundamental part of being human. I choose Jacob. He chooses me. In a world where we can and often do whatever we please, when two people make that choice it's powerful.

Merging lives with another person is an entirely different growing experience that uniquely challenges us, stretching who we are. I know because we've started that journey together already. In many ways it can seem easier than my own journey, because someone is there to encourage me on the days I simply don't have it in me to do that for myself. But it can be far more difficult because I don't have control. I must contend with another person who comes to the table with his ways of being, his past, his perspective, and then despite all that, love, support and accept him.

I had a notion that finding love was the finishing line, but now I see how naive that is. Love and commitment are some of the most complex parts of being human. It's not an ending, it's a new beginning. It's one of the most exciting and challenging experiences two people can embark on. And I'm ready for it.

15
Bad news bears

Eight months after successfully freelancing and writing during my off hours, I feel a twinge of something akin to purpose. No, I didn't get into an MFA program, but this is what a writer really does. I go to coffee shops, much like I am right now, and chip away at my book until I have important meetings with my client. My client, I still feel weird saying the words. Sometimes I tactfully avoid them so the universe is not tempted to catch on. Oh wait, did we give her a client? Why did we do that again? I imagine a secretary of some sort looking through my paperwork and finally saying, oh we did that because we want her to be a writer, remember?

"In order to write about life, first you must live it." I wrote this Ernest Hemingway quote on a post-it and stuck it onto my bathroom mirror. I wanted to see it every day, to remind myself if I live an interesting life, the rest will follow.

Earnest Hemingway never even went to college. This realization planted a seed in me. Call it fate or confirmation bias, but since then I've stumbled onto a number of materials that seem to reinforce this story. Just last week I was reading *Big Magic* by Elizabeth Gilbert. In it, she shared that grad school may not be the best place to learn to be a writer, life is the ultimate classroom. Yes, I thought excitedly as I held onto the book's pages. That's exactly it! And so, since then, I've made it my mission to experience life and let it inform my writing. Every situation, person or incident is an opportunity. *Is there something here?* is my new secondary reaction to life's inconvenient moments, many of which I've experienced right here in this very coffee shop.

MIAM is a stylish little place in the heart of Wynwood, Miami's trendiest district lined with funky art galleries, chic boutiques, late-night bars and independently owned coffee shops. Everyone here is beautiful but not in a traditional way. The beauty here is raw. This is a borough where looking interesting is more important than being pretty. That is a repressed model reserved for South Beach.

I'm here for a meeting and there's a specific reason I chose MIAM. Jacob would laugh if he saw me. Just last weekend we were in Wynwood looking for a place to grab coffee and do some work.

"How about MIAM?" he said, looking up from his phone excitedly. It's the same look he always gives when he knows he's found the perfect place and he's waiting for the acknowledgement.

"I don't want to go to that coffee shop," I said, feeling a bit like a child but still I refused to go.

"Why?" Jacob asked, his big eyes looking at me inquisitively. "It has everything you like in a coffee shop." I could see Jacob's mind at work. Sometimes, he is logical to a fault, which rubs up against my emotionally driven impulses. For him, life is a math equation that makes sense. For me, life is a feeling with no particular rhyme or reason.

"It's awkward."

"What? How is a coffee shop awkward?" he muttered to himself and yelped more options. He didn't protest because he knew at a certain point my decisions simply made no logical sense and it was best to accept that and move on.

How exactly does a coffee shop come to be awkward? And why am I here? The answer to that requires some backstory.

At the start of my freelance tenure with a creative agency in Miami's art district, MIAM meant nothing to me. It was just a new spot in the neighborhood, a welcome sign that mom and pop coffee shops were sprouting around the city. That is, until it became the place I had my most awkward interview.

I knew I was entirely wrong for the job, but I went anyway. They were looking for a camera personality. I was not comfortable in front of the camera. They were looking for someone to cover events. I hated work events with the fire of a thousand suns. But there I was in front of MIAM holding a microphone practicing lines that felt unnatural and swallowing my own hair as it whipped into my mouth from the heavy wind. It was the kind of interview that ended with me running to my car in relief of the solitude and texting Jacob three poop emojis in response to his inquiry on how it all went. Still, I felt an odd pull to the company.

Weeks later, the timing was right for a job that was more my speed: Writer. That was my own categorization. We had no titles, no assigned desks, no strings. In fact, calling it a company is a term I use rather loosely. It didn't feel like a business of any sort, but this was a selling point to me. So, I became their self-proclaimed writer and that's how our arrangement began. They were thrilled I brought a fresh energy to their dynamic and I was thrilled I got to be a paid writer.

It was love at first sight. We were a fusion of interesting characters: 10 people who worked together at one large table that resembled the tree of life with its intricate wooden designs, embedded charms and built-in lighting. It was an artwork designed specifically for this space so everyone could sit at one giant table, not individually at desks because that's so corporate.

We had wellness Tuesdays that included our resident in-house healer performing a reiki-type energy session. We put on art shows for up and coming artists just because we wanted to. Everyone was quirky in their own way. We laughed a lot together. The coffee was good. And so it went, I became smitten with this small company. It was a gravitational pull I could not ignore, and it felt right to be there, like family.

Eventually, they offered me a full-time gig. This is when things got weird. There was a small part of me that feared changing our relationship from freelance to full time would effectively kill the vibe. We were like roommates who were staying in an apartment paying month-to-month rent, our union constantly revisited and renewed, giving the illusion of freshness. I made up a story long ago that going full time does something to the psyche, both as an employee and employer. A full-time employee is harder to dismiss, and people grow complacent when a job begins to feel permanent. Though I knew better, I accepted the job.

I felt like a bird with clipped wings almost immediately. Suddenly, I couldn't come or go with the same freedom. My whereabouts were scrutinized, and all the familiar feelings of anxiety came rushing back. It stopped being about the contribution and became about clocking in time at a desk. It honestly felt like everything changed.

I can't completely blame this on my personal feelings. We were a group of 10 and everyone brought something into the cluster. Like family, we grew more comfortable over time. Fights erupted and people came into our pristine little creative space bringing their bad moods with them. Days went by when there was a stink of energy so palpable in the air, all we could do was avoid each other. And just a day later, as if the bad days before never happened, a good day would appear, and we all experienced the glimmer of those early days that were so fluid and creatively in sync. On those days we could not stay away from one another. We were so in love with each other, we floated on a cloud and congratulated ourselves for being lucky enough to work there.

We were all in a dysfunctional relationship with yo-yo moods and the promise of what this place could be keeping us there. I recently learned this inclination to stay was not about the job, it's deeper than that. I happened upon this information by chance. Jacob picked up a book about training dogs because we're thinking of adopting a pup of our own, a logical next step in our relationship. As we've become comfortable taking care of each other's needs, we decided it would be a great idea to do it for someone furry. One night, we were in bed with the nightlight on, me with a printout of my book and a pink pen making edits, him with his dog training book.

"Cris," he said, turning over suddenly. "I have to read this to you."

"Okay," I said, putting down my pages. "This must be good."

"It is a common misconception that negative reinforcement works. It doesn't. Positive reinforcement is what drives behavior, in dogs and people. However, the positive reinforcement doesn't have to outnumber the negative behaviors. A well-known example of this are people in abusive relationships. It's not the negative behavior that makes them stay, it's the positive behaviors, no matter how brief they are. That's how powerful positive reinforcement is. Cool, huh?"

I stared at him with my mouth agape. All of a sudden everything about my job made sense to me, maybe even my life. I was literally speechless.

In any case, I didn't know that back then. For me, it was good work for a good check. It only felt like a real job some days, which I came to learn was a creation of our own making.

We were given license to experiment. There was no reason for status meetings, briefs or any of the other inconveniences that weigh down the creative process at traditional agencies, like the one I had previously worked in. But we clung to these creature comforts because without them there would be chaos and a bunch of particular personalities triggering each other.

"Can I get you anything else?" A young tattooed guy comes

up to my table outside.

"No, thanks," I say smiling, looking at the very spot I interviewed on that fateful day.

I didn't know then how toxic the environment would become. A few weeks ago, our boss came in with a certain itchiness he tends to get. He only knows two modes: grazing in the field or charging like a bull. This was the latter.

"We need to take down the wall," he said, literally itching his scalp and talking quickly to us.

"What do you mean, take down the wall?" I asked, saying what was on the rest of the table's mind.

It's important to note that over time with competing personalities, exactly one half of our tree of life table moved to the room parallel to us. It was the first sign of serious concern, though at the time we all pretended it was so we could better concentrate.

"Yes, these walls are separating us!" he said, raising his voice excitedly.

Generally, that's the function of a wall, but I knew better than to state the obvious. "Why don't you guys just move back to the table. There's more than enough room," I said, a good suggestion I thought.

"No!" he said, laughing at the absurdity. "We need to tear down the wall."

And that was that. The next day two guys came with a hammer to unify both sides of the office. When the walls came down everyone felt weird. It wasn't a new airy breezeway that connected us once more to each other, it became a window into his side of the office that gave us a constant reminder of what he thought, namely, that we disappointed him on a constant basis.

The walls meant something to him and nothing to him in a way none of us could or would understand. I truly believe we each developed an affection for him akin to Stockholm Syndrome. Even now, I can't say I dislike him. In fact, I feel the opposite. I really like him. I think he may be a creative genius.

His professional legacy is the strange environment he created for us, a small laboratory— except I don't think we were ever intended to be the scientists as he empowered us to believe. He was. We were the mice. And we ran for the cheese every time, no matter how much we knew it was bait.

MIAM was our field trip. It's where the mice got taken for special talks. Conversations about whether or not we were truly happy there, yearly reviews, salary negotiations. This became the cornerstone of every awkward conversation we endured as employees.

It stopped being the kitschy coffee shop in Wynwood where hipsters went for swirls in their coffee. It could never be anything else but an extension of the lab for me, and yet I'm here today. I'm strategizing if this works for me anymore and I made a meeting with my ex-boss, now client. I was recently transitioned from full time back to contractor. A demotion in his eyes, a promotion in mine. But I'm still not sure being in this environment works for me (or anyone else).

Also, I'm positive I've just been stood up, because 45 minutes late is not his style. He's either early for a meeting or doesn't come at all, without even a text. My cold brew still tastes good but the ice has melted waiting for him. May as well drink it now. I take out my phone and text Jacob.

He stood me up.

Really? Are you sure?

Positive. No answer. It's 10:45 AM. He's not coming.

I'm sorry baby, what an asshole.

I want to be mad but instead I laugh out loud without care of who sees. Is it really his fault? I know better. This place, for better or worse, is a mirror revealing the way we each show up. Do we get to blame him? That's easy. It's harder to accept our part, the part each of us played right into making it exactly what it is.

"We're all bad news bears," he told me once a few weeks after working there. "We are the outcasts and misfits who don't fit in anywhere else."

When he first said it casually I nearly dismissed it. He did that a lot, passive aggressively pinch us where it hurt, usually right in the gut. But thinking back, he was right. It's true. I didn't fit in anywhere else. In fact, I still didn't fit in there. None of us do, which is why the place is falling apart. He knew it and he still hired each miscast soul to take up residency in his social experiment. He blew the thing up himself a long time ago.

Bad news bear, I repeated to myself. I'm a bad news bear. I still am.

16

Don't take it all so seriously

It's 2PM and we're in Granada, Spain. It's one of the many trips we're taking to plan our wedding. It's also a much-needed break for me as I figure out what to do about my job, but right now I don't have to think about any of those things. Jacob is napping. I can't sleep once I'm awake, so I'm curled up in a warm blanket and journaling.

Our Airbnb is a loft with modern red accents, the most notable of which are the kitchen cabinets. It's not my taste, but that's why I booked it. There's something about taking a break from my life and living like a different person that's always made going somewhere fun for me. Every new encounter is an opportunity to try a new me on. Could I be the girl with the red cabinets? Probably not, but I'll wear it for a weekend.

I was just thinking of Cassandra and how it's been a few years since I've sent her a long pen pal email, the kind I used to send on trips during stolen moments, like right now. We still think of each other and catch up, but as we've grown older the stretches of time between us widen. We cemented our friendship in Europe ten years ago, so I always think of her when I'm here.

There's a little witch swinging in the doorway. It's a small fixture suspended in the air right in the middle of the door. I can see her pointy black hat from behind. I saw her this morning as I made my coffee and wondered why she was there. It's July, way too early for Halloween. And then I remembered in Spain witches are good luck. They are celebrated as tiny little omens and you can often find them sold in small shops all over the country (most notably in the North). I enjoy cultural discrepancies like this one.

My friends all call me a witch, it's a title I've earned from having dreams that have come true over the years to hair raising specificity. I've predicted natural disasters, pregnancies, even brand-new people in my life. It's a gift I haven't had access to since my early twenties. There simply hasn't been space for those kinds of insights. They don't tend to come through when I'm distracted by the chase. I like that the witch is a symbol of positivity here. In the U.S. she's scary. Not to mention historically charged, Salem trials come to mind when I think of witches back home, visions of women wrongly burned alive in front of crowds. Witches are still depicted as ugly shrews, but not here. In Spain they are blessings hung year-round in the doorways of homes.

I used to have a little witch from Spain. I lost her over multiple moves from my parent's house to my college apartment and back to multiple apartments in Miami. Actually, now that I recall, I may have bought one for Cassandra once. If I see one on this trip, I think I'll get us each a replacement. I have a feeling her inner witch may have slipped through the cracks as well. She's moved around quite a bit. In fact, right now we're in very different parts of the world. She's in Abu Dhabi, where she's lived for two years, and I'm visiting Spain, very soon to get married and finally considering moving out of Miami. To my surprise, Jacob brought up the possibility of moving to Bryson City, the small mountain town in North Carolina where his grandparents live. I could hardly believe it, but I've actually been entertaining the thought.

You really never know what turns life will have in store for you. Cassandra isn't surprised we're considering the move, but then again, she never really is. She has that knowingness about her, she always did even back when we were 19 having our first coffee in Paris. We were backpacking with a group of college students (most of the group were strangers to us) and decided to skip out on the day's planned tour of the palace of Versailles. We just aren't museum people, no offense to the palace which I know for a fact is large and intricate and evokes all the grandeur of Paris in the 19th Century. Even then her and I opted to skip the big fuss in favor of a normal cup of coffee. Who knew that random, fateful decision would become a friendship that spanned space, time, moves, jobs and men. Who knew we'd be friends forever on that day? I did. But I guess that's the witch in me.

Shoot, my coffee's cold. I begin to reheat it in our bnb's very red microwave trying to figure out exactly what way to turn the knob. There we go. Counter-clockwise. Every European microwave I've come into contact with provides an opportunity to test my cat-like reflexes as they don't have a timer with numbers. That would be too easy. Instead, there's a knob you turn with a bunch of indiscriminate lines indicating at what point it will stop and ring obnoxiously. It's like an old school kitchen timer, right down to the constant ticking it makes until the big ring. I haven't seen one since my childhood, kitchens are "smart" now. So, every morning and during the country's designated nap time, I do a little dance with my microwave, so I don't wake everyone up. It requires my full attention to open the door at just the right time. And that time is… now! Nailed it.

I take a peek outside the window and see the busy streets of Granada. The South may look different from the North of Spain, the part my family is from, but the narrow alleys lined with balconies are universal here. It's busy out, mostly tourists. The locals are taking their daily nap. I should go to sleep but I just can't turn off my brain. It's during unguarded moments like this my grandmother comes to my mind.

I grab my pen and the small notebook Jacob bought me at the

start of this trip. Its baby blue cover features an astrological design with stars in orbit around a Bull, my sun sign, Taurus. I've been journaling daily, but not about this. The thing I know has been lingering in my mind and waiting for me to settle in, so it can safely come out.

My grandmother is gone. She died just three weeks ago. It hurts my throat to even say it, so I don't. I write it down. The words in black and white still feel unreal. Waves of grief have been hitting me hard, usually in private moments like this when I'm away from everyone, even Jacob. This is when I allow myself to weep silently. I don't stop the tears that well up in my eyes and start pouring down my face. Instead I open the windows to an indescribable smell this country has and I can feel her here. I can feel her hands, which were large for a woman, with long fingers. Her skin was rough from years of manual labor and using dish soap to wash them. She never cared much about beauty products. I remember she had an entire shelf of Avon creams that I'm certain were gifts from people who rode the bus with her. She never used them completely, it was a habit she carried with her from her childhood when supplies were scarce. The bottles that looked so shiny and new would accumulate dust in her bathroom. She'd only ever use a drop or none at all. So her hands were rough, and wrinkly and strong.

My grandmother's death happened at a time when there was a lot going on. Her transition to the next realm, whatever that may be, was not what I expected. Her death marked a big ending during a period of new beginnings in my life.

I was not physically present when she died; although I saw her deteriorate for years knowing the end was coming. You don't get better at that age, you get comfortable for what's next to come. I thought I had taken care of the feelings around her death long before the day came. In many ways it felt like she died years ago. I was wrong. Intellectualizing death is a concept. Experiencing loss is a very real thing, one that I haven't committed to feeling. I needed this time here in Spain and the promise of moving somewhere new and far, now more than ever.

About two weeks ago is when my mother called me to inform me of what comes next.

"We're going to have a mass for Tata," she said. "It's very simple, casual."

"Oh great, so we don't have to wear black?" I was looking through my closet for an outfit. Maybe dark jeans and a tasteful blouse? This is casual.

"Well..." she said, pausing and I assume trying to find the right words. "I'm wearing black but you can dress however you'd like."

I wore black.

I had to go shopping for a shirt, so my mom accompanied me. It was December and the stores were crowded. I hate shopping and I nearly missed my mother's fleeting comment as I walked into a dressing room. She was talking about the whole thing and I was distracted until the word casket caught my attention.

"Wait. What?" I asked. "There's a casket? I thought she was already cremated? Isn't this casual?"

"It is," she answered matter of factly. "It's totally casual, it's more like a blessing, really."

When the day finally arrived, I rode with Jacob to the church right by my parent's house. Upon entering the sacred space, which I hadn't done in easily over a decade, I saw a funeral car parked out front. It still did not dawn on me that my grandmother was in that car in her casual casket. I walked inside with all the assurance that this, despite the attire and unfortunate circumstance, was an informal mass meant to honor her life, not mourn her death. I greeted old family friends, parents of childhood friends, old coworkers of my mom's, and when my smile was met with grim faces and sincere apologies for our loss, I realized I was at a funeral for my grandmother.

It was a terribly inconvenient time to come to that fact. Tears began to fight their way through my eyes, and of course, I hadn't worn waterproof mascara because, well, you get it.

I wanted to be left alone and Jacob could tell. "Why don't we go sit down in the pews?" he whispered. I nodded and followed him to take a seat.

As we made our way there, my sister grabbed my arm and with sincere shock asked me, "Where are you going?"

"To sit?" we said in unison.

"We walk behind the casket..." she said, pointing to the eight men, my father included, who were carrying my grandmother's casket. Fuck my life.

The loud signature sounds of a Catholic mass began as if on cue. An organ playing somber notes filled the room loudly bouncing off the walls in an echo I could feel inside my body. It took me back to being a child in school, the last time I ever went to a mass because I had to. Back then, the powerful music produced such a visceral feeling in my body. I thought that was God. Now, it turns out this whole thing is anything but casual and the music is not helping. As I walked behind the casket with my sister and my mother, I saw a large photo of my grandmother at the altar surrounded by flower arrangements and all the things usually present at a funeral.

The priest spoke to us in Spanish. "Hello, my brothers and sisters, good morning. We're gathered here under somber circumstances to honor Rosalia Gutierrez."

I was listening and yet removed. It felt like watching a movie and I was playing a part I hadn't agreed to. His sermon was nice, and I was able to extract enough goodness from it, deleting the mentions of religion for myself. Even if it isn't my forte, it felt right because my grandmother was a woman of faith, she never wavered in her devotion to God despite things not going her way. I had no way of knowing if deep down she felt different about it, but around me, she accepted life as it unfolded. Whatever showed up was fine. *Dios aprieta pero no ahoga*, is a saying she would recite often to us. It translates literally to God squeezes, but he does not strangle, which sounds pretty bad. It's closer in sentiment to this phrase, which I consider its true

English equivalent, God doesn't give you more than you can handle. Whenever she said it, it made me want that to be true. If God thinks I'm strong enough to handle this, maybe I am.

These days, I don't talk to God or think of my creator the same way. As the priest continued to speak of faith, I was reaching for how to make his words land with me. I'm not Catholic, but I have faith in a source of power greater than me. I have faith this isn't the end. I don't know what comes after death. At some points I've believed different things. Reincarnation is one belief I've always played with. If we do come back, the idea that we choose everything in our life, right down to the bad stuff, is entirely possible. What if I made a soul contract with everyone I know? Perhaps we even travel together with a certain group of souls, which explains why some people's eyes are familiar and safe right away. There's a recognition there, almost as if we're meeting again. If that's the case, my grandmother is an infant right now in some part of the world, hopefully close to mine. I know we'll meet again somehow, someplace and we'll know.

"This woman was strong; she created a legacy. By having the courage to move several times in her life to different countries, she paved the way for her daughter to grow up educated, taken care of, and eventually in the right place to meet her husband. From then, there were children and this beautiful lineage continues. This all hinged on her courageous choices."

With each moment of the funeral unfolding before my very awareness, the priest did manage to surprise me. Most Catholic funerals follow a template, but to his credit and my deepest appreciation, he studied my grandmother's life and honored it by making connections I hadn't made before. Because of her life, a life lived always in a constant search of what's possible, my mother was able to meet my father, marry him and raise us in the United States.

My grandmother's first big move was to Cuba. She went by herself in search of something more during Spain's civil war, a notoriously bloody and violent time. I'd also come to learn later she was escaping a household where she felt restricted. Back in those days, families lived together for a long time. She lived with her mom, her brother and his new wife at the time, under his dominance and control. I understood that feeling of chasing my freedom all too well, on some level I've been doing it my whole life. I know exactly the feeling of needing to move on and start fresh, I've done that several times throughout my life already. In Cuba, she met a man, apparently a very handsome one. She married him, a first marriage for her in her mid-thirties and a second one for him in his early forties. Then my mom was born. Cuba began to feel less safe and my grandmother saw the familiar signs of a dictatorship forming. The tides were changing, and she knew all too well because she had already seen them in Spain. Her husband refused to go; he couldn't leave his older children behind. My grandmother went anyway.

I can't imagine the courage it took to leave that country alone, without her husband, and a toddler. In those days, she couldn't take her child without having her husband sign a waiver giving her permission to do so. She later told my mom it was the only time she saw her husband cry. What must that have been like, being in a room as I have been with my partner, only asking him to sign away his right as a father and leaving without any guarantee to see each other? As life would have it, he died a few years later, so it was the last time they ever saw one another.

Back in Spain she moved out on her own, finding an apartment in a nice area of Oviedo, the city closest to her hometown. She did this so my mom could go to a good school, and not just any school, but the private school the wealthy enrolled their children in. I'd like to think I inherited her ingenuity; she was like a cat who always fell right on her feet. This, of course, would only last a few years before her tirelessness would creep up again, leading her to the United States of America, her last big move. The land of the American Dream, true opportunity. She packed up her few belongings, her kid and sailed off to a new country again. I had forgotten about all of this. She was my grandma, she cooked for us, she knew how to do things like sow, and she was my one anchor to practicing Spanish. The priest reminded us all exactly what kind of person she was, someone who was courageous and trusted in her own ability to thrive in any unknown. Before she was who she was to me, she was just like me. Lost, searching and trying everything to live the absolute best life possible.

I am exactly where I am right now as a direct result of her choices. None of our lives would be like they are now had she not lived her life in that way.

"My brothers and sisters, it may seem like a strange time to mourn a death. Right now, we are nearing Christmas. Baby Jesus, his family and Christmas decorations surround us. Even on this altar life is shown to us fully, the beginning and the end. I know it will be a hard Christmas, but this is part of life and it is beautiful. She is not alone, she is free. And we will all be there one day."

The contrast of a casket surrounded by Christmas decorations and the nativity scene of Jesus's birth will be forever etched in my mind. Death and life, he said. It's all part of the process. I appreciate that he pointed out the natural progression of life, a cyclical experience that we will all get to go through. It doesn't have to be sad, it's beautiful how we enter the earth and leave it.

When the mass was over, we all went to my parent's house. My mom had prepared some snacks and wine for guests. My dad's cousin, who gave us a ride back after the funeral, told me this is where the experience ended for her.

"I never understand this part of funerals, the getting together part," she said, giving me a kiss on the cheek.

It really was a funeral... right down to the part where you get together after.

While mingling in a crowd of friends and family alike, I got a text. It was from one of my mom's friends.

Hey, the mariachis are coming. Are you able to let them in?

"Crap. I forgot about the mariachis," I said, looking at my phone.

"The what?" Jacob replied, somewhat concerned.

"Yeah, my mom's friend wanted to surprise her with something... different. She thought Mexican Mariachis could cheer her up."

"And, they're here... like, right now?"

"They're on their way, yes," I said defensively.

It was beginning to sink in that I agreed to this day and time because I hadn't thought this was a funeral. It was a casual mass and we'd be home just us and my parents. And now, there's a Mariachi band and I don't know how that fits into this context.

Jacob saw all the conclusions I was coming to and set his beer down. "I'll go outside and let them in the backyard," he said, rubbing my arm as he exited the front door.

I took a big sip of my wine and looked in the mirror of my parent's foyer. My hair was dark and loose, finally back to its natural brown shade after a year of growing out my highlights. My face so pale my green eyes popped more than usual. My lips were extra red, which happens when I'm sad on account of how my body heats up. I took another nervous sip thankful my red lips probably hid the wine marks I typically get. Cris, what were you thinking? This is about to get really weird for everyone. I took another gulp and it burned my throat. As I coughed to clear it, the door opened and now Jacob looked worried, which made me worried. WTF happened?

"Babe, I just had a serious talk with the singer. They are all in full Mariachi attire, like black velvet suits with big hats and glitter, the whole nine yards. They asked me to warn your mom because some of the songs may be emotional."

Everything he said should be funny, but it really wasn't.

"Do you understand?" he said, grabbing my arm again. "You need to go now."

I nodded and took another gulp of my wine. The images and sounds of Mexican Mariachis came into my mind and it was unsettling. I've only seen them a few times, but they are loud. Very loud. And their music is not a subtle melody that can play in the background of a cocktail party. Nothing about Mexican Mariachis blend in. The outfits, the songs and the instruments are meant to evoke feeling and movement in a crowd. Mariachis usually don't play long sets because of their disruption. There are trumpets and thunderous vocals. And that's all about to happen at my mother's carefully crafted casual funeral.

I walked into the living room and saw everyone in their black outfits, catching up and saying the things you say at funerals. There was care in some faces, others were excited because they probably hadn't seen each other in a long time, others were showing photos on their phones probably of kids or trips. In the sea of faces, I caught my mom. She was talking to her old friends and my stomach turned into a knot. Then, I saw my dad. Yes, I'll tell my dad and ask him to tell my mom. Better plan.

I walked up to my dad, "Hey Dad, can I talk to you in the foyer for a second."

My dad smiled and excused himself and walked over confidently and with ease. He likely thought I was going to ask him where something was in their house. It made breaking the news to him horrifying and funny, but I pushed that aside because now was not the moment to appreciate the irony. The moment I'll never forget hasn't happened yet, not by quite a bit.

"Dad," I said, taking one more sip of my wine. "I dunno how to say this so I'm just gonna say it. There are Mariachis here right now, like, fully dressed and setting up to play a short concert in our yard."

His eyes grew wide. Before he could interrupt me with all the questions a logical person would ask, I placed my hand up to stop him.

"There's more. They told us to warn mom before they begin to play because the music may be emotional and honestly I had no idea how inappropriate this would feel right now and I have no idea what else to do. But it's happening."

"But..." my dad said, I could see the sinking reality had just set in and maybe a hint of panic too.

"There's no time. I'm going to go out back, you need to tell mom right now."

And then I left my poor father who walked over to my mom with the same misleading request I made to him. They walked away to the foyer and he proceeded to drop this bomb on her lap. Her eyes grew somewhat wide with concern and then she turned it off, just like that. I saw her reassure him and proceed out to the yard to fulfill her duty, which was not to panic in front of all our guests and make this truly awkward spectacle as casual as possible. This isn't a funeral with a Mexican Mariachi band, it's a mass followed by an intimate gathering with some spirited live music. It was fascinating to behold. For a second and not longer, I wondered if this was what a nervous breakdown looked like? Would this be the catalyst that pushes my mother over the edge? Would she find herself at the grocery store in the pickle aisle suddenly having all the reactions she held in? As she tosses jars of pickles in the aisle to the horrifying dismay of onlookers, would we get that call from the manager not quite knowing how to explain? I saw a little piece of myself in her disconnection and numbness. It was oddly one of the times I felt most connected to her.

We gathered outside and my mom stood alone. My dad had left, presumably to have his own breakdown, and the optics were absurd. There was my mom surrounded by her friends, my friends, family, old colleagues and there was the Mariachi band about to sing into a microphone.

"They brought microphones?" I whispered harshly into Jacob's ear. "Fucking, really? As if Mariachi bands aren't loud enough?"

He shrugged and put his hand on my shoulder reassuringly. It was all he could do in that moment.

The lead singer began to speak. "Ma'am, are you a widow today?" Oh my fuck.

My mother laughed, "No but if my husband doesn't get out here I may well be." Now we all laughed. She was good, charming even, in a way she never accessed in life easily. It was also kind of scary to watch. Maybe her pickle moment was coming sooner than I thought.

"I'm sorry for the confusion," the singer said, straightening her large hat moving the glittery tassels from her direct line of vision. "This is an old song about lost love."

If I thought the Catholic sounds of organs were loud, that was God's small way to prepare me for the noise that was to come. The woman sang with a feeling so raw even with her voice booming over the microphone, I felt her pain. We all swayed and watched. It was truly a spectacle. Eventually my dad joined for a song, and when they announced their final song, he disappeared again. It was an unfamiliar song to me but still hauntingly beautiful.

As the trumpets blared, Jacob put his arms around me. "Didn't your grandmother hate Mexican music?"

I nearly spit out my wine and laughed. I laughed so hard I felt it in my stomach. It was a highly inappropriate reaction but at this point, no one was looking at me but Jacob. I felt it in my face which was frozen from how hard I was giggling. Jacob began to laugh. Then my sister turned around and started to laugh so hard tears streamed down her face. Cassandra looked back at the sight of us three losing our shit and then she began to laugh. And all four of us felt a truly joyful moment as our cackles filled the air along with the heavy Mexican melody. I looked up at the sky and smiled. My grandmother, even from beyond, gifted this momentary reprieve. She always did that for us.

Don't take it all so seriously. It's the last sentence I write in my notebook, her advice to me always. I look back and read the funeral story I just penned. It's a bad habit most journaling guides say not to do, but I can never help myself. I've been taking it all so seriously for years, making all my mistakes mean something about me. I begin to cry and also laugh. I sip my coffee but it's cold again and there's no part of me willing to fight the microwave, and then I laugh some more about how I even take that seriously.

Jacob comes down from the loft yawning, "*Amor*?" He looks puzzled.

I'm curled up on the couch laughing and crying by myself.

"What happened while I napped?" he says.

"I just wrote about my grandmother's funeral," I say, wiping stray tears away.

"Man, that must be a good entry," he says, kissing my forehead. "Can you read it to me?"

"You really wanna hear it?"

"Yeah of course, I always do. Want me to reheat your coffee?"

I hand it to him and begin to read, reliving the experience all over again. When I finish with that last sentence, I look back up at Jacob.

"Man, that was beautiful. You nailed it. I still can't believe there were Mariachis. I think you gotta share this."

"I dunno who would care, you know? It's funny because we were there."

"No Cris, this is actually funny. Why are you taking it all so seriously? Let go. Share it."

"Yeah, you're right. I've been holding it all in for so long and I'm tired, you know?"

"Yeah babe, I do."

"I never understood why she had that message for me. Don't take it all so seriously. I get it now. I've been doing it this entire time. I make it all matter so fucking much. I make it all mean something about who I am. I've been living in an on-and-off existential crisis since I was 20, maybe even before."

He comes over and hugs me tightly once more. "I get it babe, I do it too. I take so much so seriously, I make stuff about work and money mean something about who I am, but it's an illusion you know? Let that shit go. This is powerful," he says, pointing at my notebook. "The world gets to hear your story. Not to mention, it may be one of my favorite memories... in retrospect." He laughs.

I look back down at the funeral entry and wonder if I could actually share this.

"I'm gonna shower," he says. "Let's go have a glass of wine and some tapas."

"Okay, I'll hop in after you."

He leaves so I get up and put my notebook away. I hear the shower turn on and I begin to look around some more at this apartment that's bright and different from me. I catch myself in the mirror, which is shaped like a star. My lips are red from the crying and my hair is a curly, dark mess. I start to fix it and then I stop. Oh what the fuck, who cares?

I walk back to the window and sniff the Spanish air once more. The familiar scents of my grandmother fill my lungs. Okay, Tata. I get it now. I really do.

17
Embrace That Girl

"We are the source for everything in our lives," the blue-eyed man says to us once again. We've just taken our seats for the last time. Though it's been a few days, I still can't fully believe I'm in this strange hotel at a seminar. I'm just now starting to see the people who are shoulder to shoulder with me as peers, each of us here because something is missing, none of us better or worse than the other.

I always placed an emphasis on my thirties, how I would have everything figured out. Now that I'm here, I don't see what all the fuss is about. I feel wiser, for sure, but I still feel like a blank canvas in many ways just waiting for my next decade of evolution to etch itself onto my surface.

My twenties have been a hunt for meaning as I stubbornly gave purpose to each uncomfortable moment. There's comfort in order, even if it's outside of our realm of understanding. It's scarier to think it's all random.

And yet, as I sit here in this seminar, the resounding message is clear: nothing is random and I am creating everything. It's obvious that this, like all the other circumstances in my life, was sourced by me. I chose all of it. I chose each job and boss I ever had. I chose all my great loves and not-so-great loves. I chose my friends. I chose Jacob. I literally picked everything out just so. I did it. It wasn't magic that healed me and it wasn't the card reading that changed my life. It was me all along.

"Commit to making something happen. If you believe it, you will make it so," the man on stage continues to say. His voice feels like an echo of all the lessons that have contributed to me being in this seat right now just past my thirtieth birthday.

It's taken me so long to cross the bridge and be the person I am. And yet, it was only possible by embracing That Girl, a girl I have tried to erase, rewrite and change over the years.

The girl that keeps popping up like a thorn in my book, which I've been slowly putting together and then taking apart because a flood of ghostly memories I'd rather forget come with her. This book inside me feels like it needs to be written but I'm afraid it will never come out because I can't make peace with her. That's the secret I can't admit even now as I've told my small group at this seminar that I'm a writer.

"What are you working on?" they asked.

"A book about my twenties," I said.

And then I glossed over the glaring detail that I can't face myself. That my body goes flush with a horrific physical reaction to That Girl, my girl. She's sitting next to me right now fully visible.

I've done all but deny her existence in favor of looking good, being the kind of person I think I should be and am for all anyone else knows. I've done a good job suppressing her memory and even changing her identity to a less humiliating version of me. I'm still doing it now, even here at a seminar I willingly signed up for, lying to people about who I really am by pretending I only have manageable fears.

I thought it was working for the most part, but it wasn't. And that's why I'm here.

I've resisted her, neglected her, downright questioned her existence for most of my twenties. And yet here she remains, remarkably intact, and even more shocking, happy to see me.

My denying her existence never made her go away. She was either too chubby, emotional, naive or boring. I never realized I went through life and That Girl was right there behind my back. My denial her most abundant source of power.

She did not do this to hurt me. That Girl wanted to be acknowledged, loved and embraced. She patiently waited the better part of a decade so I could do the one thing that would make her stop getting in the way of me being who I really wanted to be: accept her.

Our ghosts are not intentionally haunting us, in fact, we are the ones who invoke their phantom presence every time we resist a part of ourselves. That Girl comes in different forms for all of us. I've seen her show up as jealousy, bad mouthing, cheating, anger, violence. That Girl is in our lives as the thing we want so badly to wish away, wish we never did or thought, that horrible thing that doesn't even feel like us, so why acknowledge it is us at all?

And yet, here she is right next to me as this man tells us to look at ourselves and what we're pretending not to know. Tears are rolling quietly down my face as I dab them with my tissue. That Girl finally has my full attention.

She is a child who can be obnoxious and defensive but only because she's responding to her most primal instincts to be loved, frustrated the rest of the world only sees her one way. She is a teenager who becomes disengaged because she cannot stand the thought of someone getting to know her and confirming she is as useless as she feels. She is a girl ashamed of her burning desire to find love, afraid it makes her pathetic and so no one will love her. She is a young adult in pain and unable to communicate, misunderstood and avoiding all the hard conversations. She is a woman that even now does not want to cry in public and show people who she really is, because maybe that's a lot to handle.

"Go towards what makes you uncomfortable. Your power is

there. It is the very thing that will give you what you desire most," our orator says, taking a seat on stage. The lights go dim and I hear an entire room of people sniffing.

I know when this is over and I leave, I'm going to run towards That Girl in the shape of my book. The story I've been so painfully fearful of writing. I'm going to leave this place and write her exactly as she is, mistakes and all. I have given That Girl so many touch ups over the years, a little optimism infused here, a few insecurities removed there, some minor deletions and edits.

This is the only time in my life I've ever loved her and the only time I don't feel her lingering behind me. I feel a sense of release and pride and rawness that comes from being seen— for real. I understand what That Girl has gifted me. She's given me all the circumstances I needed to become who I am. She isn't pitiful, she's courageous and powerful. She didn't besmirch my reputation or hold me back from my amazing life, she is the reason for everything good in my life. All the stories I told myself about her were wrong all these years.

Because none of the stories we tell ourselves are true at the end of the day. Maybe a universal power or God really does exist as a guiding force, or maybe, just maybe, I am the one responsible for everything.

So here I am, thirty, about to walk out of a seminar at this strange run-down hotel by Miami International Airport. It's somehow become the place I'd look That Girl right in the eyes and give her the hug of all hugs, the type of embrace that knocks the wind out of you with its sincerity. I tell her she is whole, perfect and complete, that I love her no matter what she's done or failed to do, that I applaud her for getting this far and that she deserves unconditional love, that I am not thriving despite her, but because of her.

It's taken me this decade to come to the most powerful conclusion of all. I can believe life is constantly happening to me or I can believe that I am the source.

I choose to be the author.
I created it.
I set it all up.

ABOUT THE AUTHOR

Photograph of the author by Nicole McConville

Cris Ramos Greene is a Spanish-American writer and author of *Embrace That Girl*. With a decade of blogging about travel, dating and the human condition, Cris has a uniquely wry voice that shines through her debut book.

A lifelong writer, Cris first began creating layered characters who find the humor in heartbreak during high school. She has a B.S. in Public Relations from the University of Florida and still bleeds blue and orange. After 10 years of working in Miami's art scene and ad world, she penned her first book and moved to The Smoky Mountains.

Cris lives and works out of her cozy home in Bryson City, NC where she is accompanied by her husband Jaime and pup Bo. She can be found sipping wine every weekday at 5pm on her porch.

Sign up for her newsletter at thecrisramos.com

Follow her on instagram @crisrgreene

CPSIA information can be obtained
at www.ICGtesting.com
Printed in the USA
BVHW032325140920
588318BV00005BA/18